FINDING FREEDOM
IN A
SEX-OBSESSED
WORLD

NEIL T. ANDERSON

HARVEST HOUSE PUBLISHERS

EUGENE, OREGON

Cover by Terry Dugan Design, Minneapolis, Minnesota

FINDING FREEDOM IN A SEX-OBSESSED WORLD
The Bondage Breaker® Series
Some material previously released in *A Way of Escape*
Copyright © 2004 by Neil T. Anderson
Published by Harvest House Publishers
Eugene, Oregon 97402
www.harvesthousepublishers.com

Harvest House Publishers, Inc., is the exclusive licensee of the federally registered trademark THE BONDAGE BREAKER.

Library of Congress Cataloging-in-Publication Data
Anderson, Neil T., 1942–
    Finding freedom in a sex-obsessed world / Neil T. Anderson.
        p. cm. — (The bondage breaker series)
    Includes bibliographical references.
    ISBN 0-7369-1298-3 (pbk.)
    1. Chastity. 2. Sex—Religious aspects—Christianity. 3. Lust—Religious aspects—Christianity.
I. Title. II. Series.
    BV4647.C5A557   2004
    241'.66—dc22   2003018062

Printed in the United States of America

04 05 06 07 08 09 10 11 12 / VP-MS / 10 9 8 7 6 5 4 3 2

To my wife, Joanne

You are my helpmate, best friend, and confidante.
I love you.

Acknowledgments

You are to be commended for picking up this book. It shows you have the courage to face the truth with a desire to find your freedom in Christ, or that of someone you love.

The time it took to write this book was but a fraction of the time I have spent with hurting people. Most have been victims of sexual abuse, and many have been carried away by their lusts, enticed by a world spiraling out of control into a cesspool of sexual madness. Many of the abused have become abusers. They have all borne the shame of a defiled temple and cringed under the accusations of the evil one. They are your sons and daughters, spouses, friends, and co-workers. If you heard their story, you would weep with them.

I want to thank my friend, Dr. Charles Mylander, for reading this manuscript and writing the foreword. The editorial staff at Harvest House Publishers has always been a delight to work with. You have helped me be a better writer.

Finally, I want to thank my wife, Joanne, who reads all my manuscripts, and to whom I have dedicated this book.

Contents

For Those Who Are Struggling

I WISH THIS POWERFUL BOOK had been mine when I was going through my own savage struggle with lustful thoughts. For years they plagued my mind and irritated my soul. I tried everything I thought a Christian should try—Bible study and memorization, new experiences with God, and efforts at self-discipline—but nothing seemed to work for long.

I prayed during those times of struggle, too—God knows I prayed. I repented and turned away from my sins more often than I can remember. God answered my prayers at the moment. But the lustful thoughts always came back. Although I did not fall into an adulterous affair and avoided pornography like the plague, lust was the battleground of my Christian experience. I took three steps forward and two steps back, then two steps forward and three steps back, and then one step forward and four steps back.

Yes, there were holy-ground moments of fresh victory before God. I loved them. But then came the agonizing weeks and months of defeat. I hated them and hated my sin, yet I could not escape it. Romans 7 describes my experience perfectly. I studied the message of Romans 6 and 8 and tried to apply it. Somehow it worked in every area of my life except one. I could not seem to live constantly in the Spirit when it came to lust. There was something compulsive about my thought life that felt abnormal to me. Little did I know how real the spiritual problem truly was.

During these years of silent, hidden struggle I felt I had no one to talk to. Later I figured out that there was no one I *wanted* to talk to. My pride and my shame almost did me in. I described my turning point in my book *Running the Red Lights*. That turning point was effective in setting me free in Christ, but now I know it was unnecessary for me to have waited so long.

This book's simple insight of renouncing every sexual use of my body and mind outside of marriage proved so helpful when I first heard it. My temptations were much more normal by that time, and the compulsiveness was already broken. Nevertheless, as I asked Christ to bring to my mind each instance of sexual sin, three vivid memories popped into my thoughts. Each one was, I now believe, a foothold Satan and his demons used to form a stronghold in my mind. Renouncing each one led to greater freedom and joy than ever before.

In the days of my greatest struggle I did not know about the activity of Satan in putting his evil thoughts in my mind. I did not know my true identity as a man who was crucified, buried, made alive, raised up, and seated with Christ (Galatians 2:20; Romans 6:4; Ephesians 2:4-6). I did not know how to apply God's grace and truth to take every thought captive in obedience to Christ. I did not understand the authority and influence over the evil one that is mine in Christ. The Lord did teach me many lessons about becoming a winner and overcoming lust, but if I had had this book back then, Christ would have set me free years sooner.

Most Christians desperately need this message, either for their present struggle or for something in their past that has not been resolved. Any good book is like a cherry pie. Some readers will always find a theological pit and then be tempted to throw away the whole pie. Please don't do that. The message of this book has the potential to show millions of people how Christ can set them free from sexual bondage. Read it, pass it on, and spread the word.

Dr. Charles Mylander
Executive Director of Evangelical
Friends Mission

You Can Experience Freedom

RICK'S LIFE WAS AN ENDLESS QUEST FOR INTIMACY. As a child, he was sexually abused by his grandmother after his father committed suicide. As a young man, he embarked on a desperate search to fill the void in his life. After marrying his college sweetheart, Emily, he kept trying to cover his bitterness and pain with extramarital sexual encounters, excessive work, and the approval of others—but to no avail. Emily lost patience with him and left.

While listening to a tape by Dr. Charles Stanley, Rick fell to his knees and asked Jesus to save him from himself and from the sin that never delivered what it promised. He and his wife were reconciled, and together they bore four children. To others they appeared to be a respectable Christian family.

Rick, however, was still haunted by the lies that his needs for acceptance, security, and significance could somehow be met by satisfying his lusts for sex, food, social acceptance, and affirmation at work. He fell back into his old patterns of immorality. He was sexually involved with numerous partners, including a married woman, while continuing to play the role of the Christian husband and father. His double life left his soul in turmoil.

Devastated by the breakup of an affair, Rick confessed everything to his family and entered a three-month inpatient program for his addictions. Emily was crushed and told him not to return home. The divorce that followed prompted Rick to make an attempt at renewing his faith in Christ. He prayed and committed himself to not get involved sexually during his 90 days of treatment. His continuing belief that the right woman would meet his deep and seemingly unquenchable need for love only led to more failure, though. While he continued doing daily devotions, seeking God's guidance, and "witnessing" to his co-workers, he was involved with yet another married woman.

For years Rick rode a spiritual and emotional roller coaster. His convictions would drive him to break off relationships and return to the Lord. Then personal problems and depression would lead him back to the same old flesh patterns of sex and food. He felt powerless to control his behavior.

> The "pimp" in my mind repeatedly promised me fulfillment if I would only prostitute myself one more time. But he never fulfilled his promise. Life for me was like pushing a car. When things were going all right, it required only a little effort. But every time I tried to push the car over the mountain of my sexual bondage, the car rolled back over me—leaving me desperate, hurt, and without hope again. I couldn't stop this cycle no matter how much I sought God. My sexual addiction ruled everything in my life. I hated it, I knew it was destroying me from the inside out—but I kept heeding the pimp in my mind again and again.

Rick's godly mother encouraged him to attend our ministry's "Living Free in Christ" conference. During the first evening of the conference he was harassed by sexual fantasies in his mind. However, he did hear one statement that gave him some hope: "If the Son sets you free, you will be free indeed" (John 8:36). Rick says, "I knew I wasn't free. I was powerless to stop the fruitless search for fulfillment and satisfaction in sex, food, and work."

Rick made an appointment to meet with me privately during the conference:

I knew while driving to the meeting that something was going to happen. My heart felt like it was going to explode. There was a war raging within me. The pimp in my mind, who had controlled my life for years, didn't want me to go. But I was determined to experience the freedom Neil talked about.

I expected Neil to slap me on the side of the head and shout out an exorcistic prayer. Then I would surely fall to the floor and flap around uncontrollably until the effects of his prayer set me free. It didn't happen that way. Neil listened quietly as I shared my story, then he said in a calm voice, "Rick, I believe you can be free in Christ."

As Neil led me through the Steps to Freedom in Christ, I could hear the pimp's insistent lies in my mind. The inner battle was intense, but I was ready for the shackles to be broken. So I repented of my sin, renounced all the lies I had believed, renounced every sexual use of my body as an instrument of unrighteousness, and forgave all those who had offended me. As I did, peace began to roll in and drown out 37 years' worth of lies. I sensed a holy silence in my mind. The pimp was gone and, praise God, I was free!

Rick's freedom was tested right away. The next day during the conference he was bombarded by immoral thoughts. But he took those thoughts captive to the obedience of Christ and chose to believe the truth that he was a child of God, alive and free in Christ. That night he was tempted to pursue another destructive relationship. He called upon the Lord, and the "holy silence" returned.

Rick has since experienced a genuine and growing relationship with his heavenly Father. He stopped watching the raunchy television programs and movies that played a large part in feeding his lustful habits. He had a desire to study the Bible and pray now that he was experiencing his freedom in Christ.

Every Child of God Can Find Freedom

Every child of God in sexual bondage, and those who have been sexually exploited by others, can be set free from their past and experience their freedom in Christ. Only then can they continue in the process of being conformed to the image of God. Jesus broke the power of sin on the cross, defeated the devil, made us new creations in Him, and set us free from our past so we can be all He created us to be. This truth can be appropriated by anyone who puts their trust in God and genuinely repents of their sins.

I tell Rick's story to offer you some hope and to illustrate that nobody's problem is just a sex problem. Secular treatment centers and a myriad of self-help programs offered Rick no success solving his sexual addiction, which was bundled together with his early childhood experiences and every other aspect of his life. For him, sexual promiscuity was a self-gratifying attempt to be somebody. When we try to find self-verification through appearance, performance, or social status in this fallen world, we will fail. People don't have sex problems, or alcohol problems, or marriage problems—they have life problems. All our problems are inextricably bound up in our relationships with God, the god of this world, and our family, friends, neighbors, and co-workers. Sex is not just a physical phenomenon, it is integrally related to our souls, and is part of our spirituality.

I also want to make it clear that I did not set Rick free. Nor did the Steps to Freedom in Christ,* which are just a tool that gives structure to the repentance process of helping people submit to God and resist the devil (James 4:7). Knowing the truth, followed by genuine repentance, is what set Rick free. Only Jesus can set the captive free and bind up the brokenhearted. Rick is not a sexual pervert, adulterer, or fornicator—he is a child of God, a joint heir with Jesus, and a new creation in Christ. Knowing his identity and position in Christ is what

* See chapter 8 for more information on the Steps.

enables him to live a righteous life by faith in the power of the Holy Spirit.

In this book we will consider our sexuality in light of God's original plan in creation. Then we will discuss the effects of the fall and how sin perverts our character and understanding. We will look at some Old Testament guidelines for sexual purity and marriage and explain why nobody could live a righteous life under the law. I will use the story of David to illustrate the downward spiral to sexual bondage. Finally, we will discuss God's answer for sexual freedom and purity under the covenant of grace. Every child of God is alive and free in Christ, and every one of us can experience our freedom if we know the truth and are willing to repent. May the good Lord enable you to do just that.

CHAPTER ONE

Trouble in the Garden

Human sexuality is too noble and beautiful a thing,
too profound a form of experience, to turn
into a mere technique or physical relief,
or a foolish and irrelevant pastime.

J.V.L. CASSERLEY

GOD REVEALED HIS PLAN FOR THE SEXUAL LIFE and health of humanity in the creation account recorded in Genesis 2:18,21-25:

> The LORD God said, "It is not good for the man to be alone. I will make a helper suitable for him."...So the LORD God caused the man to fall into a deep sleep; and while he was sleeping, he took one of the man's ribs and closed up the place with flesh. Then the LORD God made a woman from the rib he had taken out of the man, and he brought her to the man.
> The man said, "This is now bone of my bones and flesh of my flesh; she shall be called 'woman,' for she was taken out of man." For this reason a man

will leave his father and mother and be united to
his wife, and they will become one flesh.

The man and his wife were both naked, and
they felt no shame.

God created Adam in His own image and breathed life into
him, and Adam became spiritually and physically alive. Something was missing, however. It wasn't good for Adam to be
alone—he needed a suitable helpmate. None of the animals
God had created could adequately fulfill Adam's need nor have
a complementary relationship with him. So God created Eve
from Adam's rib.

The new couple was naked and unashamed. There were no
dirty or offensive parts of their body. Intimate sexual relationships were not separate from their relationship with God. There
was no sin and nothing to hide, so Adam and Eve had no reason
to cover up their nakedness.

The purpose and responsibility of this first couple was to "be
fruitful and increase in number; fill the earth and subdue it"
(Genesis 1:28). Sex was intended for procreation as well as pleasure. They didn't "make" love. Sexual intercourse and physical
touch were the means by which the two could express their love
to each other and multiply. They were afforded a tremendous
amount of freedom as long as they remained in a dependent
relationship with God. They had a perfect life and could have
lived forever in the presence of God. All their needs were provided for.

The Fall and Its Results

Satan was also present in the universe. The Lord had commanded Adam and Eve not to eat from the tree of the knowledge
of good and evil or they would die (Genesis 2:17). Satan ques-
tioned and twisted God's command and tempted Adam and Eve
through the same three channels of temptation that exist today:
"the lust of the flesh and the lust of the eyes and the boastful

pride of life" (1 John 2:16 NASB). Deceived by the craftiness of Satan, Eve defied God and ate the forbidden fruit, and Adam chose to follow her in her defiance and eat also.

At that moment, Adam and Eve died spiritually, meaning that their intimate relationship with God was severed. Their souls were no longer in union with Him. Many years later, they died physically, which is also a consequence of sin (Romans 5:12). Their perfect life in the garden was ruined by their choice to sin. Filled with guilt and shame, "the eyes of both of them were opened, and they realized they were naked; so they sewed fig leaves together and made coverings for themselves...and they hid from the LORD God among the trees of the garden" (Genesis 3:7,8).

The fall affected Adam and Eve's life in many ways. First, *it darkened their minds*. Trying to hide from God revealed they had lost a true understanding of who their Creator was, since no one can hide from an omnipresent God. They were darkened in their understanding because they were separated from the life of God (Ephesians 4:18). Even today the natural person cannot understand spiritual things, "because they are spiritually discerned" (1 Corinthians 2:14).

Second, *the fall affected their emotions*. The first emotion expressed by Adam and Eve after the fall was fear. When God came looking for the pair, Adam said to Him, "I was *afraid* because I was naked; so I hid" (Genesis 3:10). To this day, anxiety disorders are the number-one mental health problem of the world, and "fear not" is the most repeated command in Scripture.

Those who live in guilt and shame want to hide and cover up. Fear drives them away from any kind of exposure of their inner world. Without God's unconditional love and acceptance, they run from the light or try to discredit its Source. Unable to live up to God's eternal standards of morality, they face the prospect of continuing to live in guilt and shame, or like Adam, they blame someone else (Genesis 3:12).

Third, *the fall also affected Adam and Eve's will.* Before they sinned, they could make only one wrong choice: to eat from the tree of the knowledge of good and evil, which was forbidden. Every other choice they could make in the garden was a good choice. However, because Adam and Eve made that one bad choice, after that they were confronted every day with many good *and* bad choices—just as we are today. We can choose to pray or not pray, believe God or not believe Him. We can choose to yield or not yield to a variety of temptations presented to us by the world, the flesh, and the devil. Sexual bondage is the result of wrong choices.

We Need the Light

As a result of the fall, we are totally helpless and have no hope of escaping the bondage of sin without God. No person living independently of God can live a righteous life or withstand the conviction of His perfect light.

> Everyone who does evil hates the light, and will not come into the light for fear that his deeds will be exposed. But whoever lives by the truth comes into the light, so that it may be seen plainly that what he has done has been done through God (John 3:20-21).

The first step in recovery for anyone in sexual bondage is to come out of hiding in the darkness and face the truth in the light. Many people have told me they want to get out of sexual bondage because they are tired of living a lie. Bondage to sex is one of the easiest things to lie about. For example, the effects of food addiction (overeating, anorexia, or bulimia) are revealed by our physical appearance. Drug or alcohol addiction will affect our performance, which is noticeable to others. Those living in sexual bondage, however, have few obvious clues others can see—unless they are exposed or contract some sexually transmitted disease. You can be the president of the United States and be sexually addicted, but I doubt you could be the president if you were chemically addicted. Tragically, those who are chemically addicted are often sexually addicted as well, but they usually will not seek treatment for their sexual addiction unless they are exposed.

A Rebel Usurps Authority

When Adam and Eve sinned, Satan usurped their dominion over the earth and became the god of this world. When Jesus was tempted, Satan offered Him the kingdoms of the world if He would bow down and worship him (Luke 4:6). Jesus didn't dispute Satan's claim to earthly spiritual authority and even referred to him as "the prince of this world" (John 12:31; 14:30; 16:11). Paul called Satan "the prince of the power of the air" (Ephesians 2:2 NASB). As a result of Adam and Eve's fall, "the whole world is under the control of the evil one" (1 John 5:19).

The good news is that God's plan of redemption was under way immediately upon Satan's wresting authority from Adam and Eve. The Lord cursed the serpent and foretold the downfall of Satan (Genesis 3:14-15), which was accomplished by Christ on the cross. Ultimate authority in heaven and earth belong to Jesus. Satan's days of ruling over the kingdoms of this world are numbered.

Because we are physical descendants of Adam and Eve, all of us are born spiritually dead and live under the dominion of Satan. But when we receive Christ, we are transferred from Satan's kingdom to God's kingdom (Colossians 1:13; Philippians 3:20). Satan is still the ruler of this world, but he is no longer *our* ruler. Jesus Christ is the Lord of our lives. The deceiver can't do anything about our position in Christ—but if he can get us to believe that our identity and position in Christ aren't true, we will live as though they aren't.

Even as members of Christ's kingdom we are still vulnerable to Satan's accusations, temptations, and deceptions. If we give in to his schemes, Satan can influence our thinking and behavior. And if we remain under his influence long enough and fail to resist him, Satan will gain a measure of control in our lives. Much of his dominance is sexual.

That's what happened to Rick, whose story we heard in the introduction. Before he became a Christian, he made sinful choices that led to sexual bondage. He hadn't recovered from his sexual abuse and chose to be sexually promiscuous. After Rick gave his life to Christ, the pimp in his mind had him convinced that immoral sex was still the answer to his search for love. Only after Rick understood his identity in Christ and exercised his authority in Him was he able to silence the pimp's lies and break free of his sexual bondage.

The Seeds of Sexual Bondage

Most of the people who come to our ministry are struggling with some kind of sexual problem. The ongoing cosmic battle between God's kingdom and the kingdom of darkness is often manifested in sexual sin because sex is the means by which the seeds of reproduction are sown in either kingdom.

Christians who respect and obey God's directives in Scripture regarding sexual purity are sowing seeds in the kingdom of God that will reap a harvest of peace and righteousness. People who ignore God's call to sexual purity are sowing seeds in Satan's kingdom and will reap a harvest of pain and heartache. The fruit of the seeds sown in these two kingdoms greatly impacts our world and our family relationships. Adultery and incest destroy ministries and tear up families for generations.

One of Satan's primary weapons for ruining relationships is sexual impurity. More Christian marriages and ministries are destroyed through sexual misconduct than for any other reason. People who are living in secret sexual bondage have no joy in marriage or ministry. Conversely, believers who pursue a life of moral purity are bearing fruit in the kingdom of God. The result is a positive impact for righteousness on their marriages, children, friends, and co-workers.

The strong link between Satan's kingdom of darkness and sexual bondage was illustrated to me during one of my conferences. David was referred to us by the pastoral staff of the host church. He was a successful businessman who appeared to have everything going for him. However, his wife had just left him because of his pornography addiction. One of our staff met with him to take him through the Steps to Freedom in Christ.

As we lead people through the Steps, we sometimes discern that they need to renounce any previous involvement in satanic or occult activities, even if they don't remember any. As David renounced making any covenants with Satan, he was shaken to the core when the Lord revealed to him an experience from his past. He recalled a nightmarish encounter with a spiritual being, who offered him all the sex and girls he wanted if he would just tell it he loved it. At first David refused, not sure if he was awake or dreaming. Then he gave in and said he loved Satan. Sowing that seed in Satan's kingdom resulted in the sexual bondage that was ruining David's life and marriage.

God's Design

Perversion of God's design for both reproduction and sexual relations is rampant wherever the kingdom of darkness flourishes. In the Old Testament, pagans honored Molech, a detestable Semitic deity, by the fiery sacrifice of their children—their seed—a practice God strictly prohibited (Leviticus 18:21; 20:1-5). There were many other pagan gods in biblical times whose worship involved sexual perversity. Chemosh, the national deity of the Moabites, required the sacrifice of children, and Diana of Ephesus had an explicitly sexual nature. Devotion to *anyone* or *anything* other than our Creator God is idolatry, and idolatry always leads to some perversion of moral purity.

Sexual perversion precipitated the fall of Rome. How close is America coming to a similar demise? Pornography used to be hard to find, but now every hotel room is a porno parlor—and so is every office at work or room in our homes that has a computer connected to the Internet. Canada is moving rapidly to legalize homosexual "marriages." The same effort is under way in the United States, and movies and television programs are portraying homosexual individuals and couples as the "liberated" ones who must set straight the "unenlightened." Anybody standing for traditional sexual morality is considered a bigot or "homophobe."[1]

However, the devil has never been able to do more than temporarily stop God's plan for propagating morally pure children of God and filling the earth with them. After the fall, God countered Satan's offensive by presenting a plan for redemption through the seed of the woman (Genesis 3:15). Satan was behind Pharaoh's order to kill all the male babies in Egypt when God was raising up Moses to deliver His people (Exodus 1–2).

When Christ was born, Herod issued a decree that all male babies under the age of two were to be killed. But as Matthew reports (2:7-23), the Lord told Joseph about the plot in a dream, and he took Mary and the infant Jesus to Egypt. (Today, as we watch the heartless aborting of millions of unborn children in the name of "choice," we have to wonder what great deliverance God has in store for His people and ask, "What is Satan trying to hinder this time?")

Unable to prevent the birth of the Messiah, Satan prompted Judas, one of the Lord's own disciples, to betray Him. That devious plan played right into God's hand. The grave could not hold Jesus, and His resurrection sealed Satan's fate forever.

Satan is a defeated foe. In spite of today's perversion of sex and reproduction, we can have hope. God has a plan, and it will succeed.

CHAPTER TWO

God Has a Plan

—

*When sex is divided from love there is
a feeling that one has been stopped at the
vestibule of the castle of pleasure.*

FULTON SHEEN

GOD CREATED US AS SEXUAL BEINGS—male and female. Our gender is determined at conception, and our entire sexual anatomy is present at birth. The molecular structure of a skin sample—even that of an infant—will reveal our sex, as will our saliva (female athletes are gender-tested by taking a sample of it from their mouths). God is not anti-sex; He created sex! David proclaimed, "You created my inmost being; you knit me together in my mother's womb. I praise you because I am fearfully and wonderfully made; your works are wonderful" (Psalm 139: 13-14).

Viewing sex as evil is not an appropriate response to what God created and pronounced good. "Everything God created is good, and nothing is to be rejected if it is received with thanksgiving, because it is consecrated by the word of God and prayer" (1 Timothy 4:4-5). On the other hand, Satan is evil, and sin distorts what God created. Denying our sexuality and fearing open discussion about our sexual development is playing into the devil's hand. We need to tell our congregations and our families the truth about our sexual nature and help them all live morally pure lives.

A Plan for the Ages

God's ideal plan for marriage was outlined in the Garden of Eden before Adam and Eve sinned: "A man will leave his father and mother and be united to his wife, and they will become one flesh" (Genesis 2:24). A monogamous and heterosexual marriage under God was the divine intention—one man and one woman forming an inseparable union and living in dependence upon God.

Adam and Eve were also commanded by God to procreate and fill the earth with their offspring. Had they never sinned, perhaps the world today would be populated with a race of sinless people living in perfect harmony. But Adam and Eve's sin in the garden marred God's beautiful plan. Lest we be too hard on them, however, had any of us been in the garden instead of them, we probably would have done the same thing. Adam and Eve enjoyed ideal conditions, lived in perfect light, and still sinned. We would have done no better.

Despite the fall, God did not abandon His plan for the man and the woman and their sexual relationship. Rather, He selected the procreative process of human marriage as the vehicle for redeeming fallen humanity. God covenanted with Abraham, saying, "In your seed all the nations of the earth shall be blessed, because you have obeyed My voice" (Genesis 22:18 NASB). The "seed," or descendant, God was talking about was Christ (Galatians 3:16), who would bless the whole world by providing salvation through His death and resurrection.

There was another facet to God's plan for marriage in redemptive history. The covenant relationship of marriage between husband and wife is a God-ordained picture of the covenant relationship between God and His people. The church is called the bride of Christ (Revelation 19:7), and God desires to receive to Himself a bride who is holy and blameless, "without stain or wrinkle or any other blemish" (Ephesians 5:26-27). The purity and faithfulness of a Christian marriage is to be an object lesson of the purity and faithfulness God desires in our relationship with Him.

The Bible prohibits sexual immorality for two interrelated reasons. First, unfaithfulness or sexual sin violates God's plan for the sanctity of human marriage. When you become sexually involved with someone other than your spouse—whether physically, or mentally through lust and fantasy—you shatter God's design. You bond with that person, thus blemishing the "one man and one woman" image, and you break the covenant with your spouse (1 Corinthians 6:16-17). We were created to become one flesh with only one other person of the opposite sex. When you commit sexual sin with another, you become one flesh physically and mentally, resulting in sexual bondage. That's why Paul calls this a sin against your own body.

Second, when you commit adultery, you deface the image of God's covenant relationship with His people, which your marriage was designed to portray. Think about it: A loving, pure, committed relationship between a husband and wife is God's illustration to the world of the loving, pure, committed relationship He desires with His body, the church. Every act of sexual immorality among His people tarnishes that image.

The Plan in the Old Testament

Not many generations passed before the descendants of Abraham found themselves in bondage to Egypt. God raised up Moses to deliver His people and provide them a law to govern their relationships in the Promised Land, including their sexual relationships. Six of the ten commandments listed in Exodus 20 touched on marital fidelity.

1. *You shall have no other gods before me* (verse 3). Sexual sin violates this commandment because it elevates sexual pleasure above our relationship with God. God is a jealous God. He won't tolerate a rival, including the god of our impure appetites.

2. *Honor your father and your mother* (verse 12). Sin of any kind, including sexual sin, brings shame and dishonor to your parents.

3. *You shall not commit adultery* (verse 14). God ordained sex to be confined to marriage. Adultery—sex outside of marriage—is a sin against your marriage partner and God (Genesis 39:9).

4. *You shall not steal* (verse 15). Adulterers rob their spouses of the intimacy of their relationship and steal sexual pleasure from their illicit partners.

5. *You shall not give false testimony* (verse 16). Marriage is a covenant made before God and human witnesses. Sexual sin breaks the marriage vow. In effect, the unfaithful partner lies about being faithful to his or her spouse. Adulterers often continue lying to cover up their sin.

6. *You shall not covet* (verse 17). To covet is to desire something that doesn't belong to you. All sexual sin begins with a desire for someone that is not rightfully yours.

Though most are written in the negative, the commandments of God are not restrictive—they are protective. God's intention was to prevent a fallen humanity from sowing more seeds of destruction through sexual immorality and thus enlarging the realm of the kingdom of darkness.

God's law also specified heterosexuality and condemned homosexuality. His people were to maintain a clear distinction between a man and a woman even in appearance: "A woman must not wear men's clothing, nor a man wear women's clothing, for the LORD your God detests anyone who does this" (Deuteronomy 22:5).

Homosexual marriages and sexual relations were also clearly forbidden: "Do not lie with a man as one lies with a woman; that is detestable" (Leviticus 18:22); in 20:13, "If a man lies with a man as one lies with a woman, both of them have done what is detestable. They must be put to death; their blood will be on their own heads." (Rather than stone such a person to death, in the 2003 case of Gene Robinson, an apostate church made him a bishop! A gracious church would love the man but hate the sin—and work to restore his fallen nature.)

God commanded Adam and Eve and their descendants to multiply and fill the earth. The only way they could obey that command was to procreate through the means of sexual intercourse as men and women. Men can't have children by men, and women can't have children by women. The debased lifestyle of homosexuality is in direct conflict with God's plan of populating the earth, and He detests it.

God also instructed His people regarding the spiritual purity of their marriages:

> You shall not intermarry with [pagan nations]; you shall not give your daughters to their sons, nor shall you take their daughters for your sons. For they will turn your sons away from following Me to serve other gods; then the anger of the LORD will be kindled against you, and He will quickly destroy you (Deuteronomy 7:3-4 NASB).

Ironically, the most glaring example of disobedience to this command is found in the man reputed to be the wisest who ever lived. King Solomon had 700 wives and 300 concubines, including some from the nations with whom God expressly prohibited intermarriage (1 Kings 11:1-2). "His wives turned his heart away after other gods; and his heart was not wholly devoted to the LORD his God" (11:4 NASB). We cannot have

God-honoring marriages if we seek spouses who are not children of God.

When I studied in Israel, I saw a memorial of what happens to the kingdom of God when the king violates God's commandments. Outside the walled city of Jerusalem is a place called "the hill of shame." It was on this hill that King Solomon allowed his foreign wives to build temples to other gods. Israel divided into two nations after the death of Solomon and never returned to the prominence it once enjoyed. The hill is still barren and stands as a silent reminder of the fruit of disobedience.

The Old Testament also assures us that God designed sex within the confines of marriage for pleasure as well as procreation. The Song of Solomon portrays the joys of physical love in courtship and marriage. Furthermore, the law directed that the first year of marriage should be reserved for marital adjustment and enjoyment: "When a man takes a new wife, he shall not go out with the army nor be charged with any duty; he shall be free at home one year and shall give happiness to his wife whom he has taken" (Deuteronomy 24:5 NASB).

Satan's Assault

Satan's assault on God's design of heterosexuality is evident in the account of Sodom and Gomorrah. When angels appearing as men visited Lot in Sodom, all the men of the city, young and old, clamored to have them brought outside for a homosexual orgy. God cut off this evil seed-line by destroying the two cities with fire (Genesis 19:1-29). Even today we use the term *sodomy* to describe unnatural acts of sexual intercourse, such as oral and anal sex between males.

Israel continued to battle idolatry—and the sexual immorality that always attends it—throughout Old Testament history. When Israel split into two kingdoms—Israel and Judah—both nations degenerated spiritually and morally, despite the commandments of the law and the warnings of the prophets. Both nations were judged for their sins. God raised up Assyria to destroy Israel, and Judah was conquered by Babylon and taken into exile.

The Old Testament ends on a sad note. Only a remnant of God's people returned from captivity to the land God had given them. For 400 years the stronger neighbor nations pushed them around like puppets. On the eve of Christ's birth, the Jews were in political bondage to Rome and in spiritual bondage to their apostate leaders. The glory of God had departed from Israel. It must have appeared to many that Satan had completely foiled God's plan.

But God still had a plan. Even though the moral and spiritual fabric of Israel had been shredded, He miraculously preserved the seed of Abraham: the Redeemer who would sit upon the throne of David. Abraham's seed—Jesus Christ—was about to make His entrance (John 1:14). The blessing of Abraham was soon to be extended to all the nations of the world in Christ.

God's Plan Under the New Covenant

God's plan for Christian marriages after the cross—in a world still saturated by the darkness of sin—is given in 1 Thessalonians 4:3-5:

> This is the will of God, your sanctification; that is, that you abstain from sexual immorality; that each of you know how to possess his own vessel in sanctification and honor, not in lustful passion, like the Gentiles who do not know God (NASB).

The word "possess" means to acquire or take for yourself. The word "vessel" is translated "wife" in 1 Peter 3:7. Thus verse 4 could read, "That each of you know how to take a wife for himself in sanctification and honor." God's plan is the same in the New Testament as it was in the Old Testament: monogamous, heterosexual marriages under Him that are free of sexual immorality.

My first attempt at discipling a young college man failed miserably. No matter how I tried to help him, he couldn't seem to get his spiritual life together. I was baffled. During that time, he was dating one of the nicest young Christian women in the college group. Finally we stopped our futile attempt at discipleship.

Two years later he confessed to me that, while I had been trying to disciple him, he had been sleeping with several coeds, though not with the woman he had been dating. He admitted he had written me off after he had heard me talk about sexual purity. He wanted to be a growing Christian, but he wasn't about to give up his sexual lifestyle. It was little wonder my attempt to disciple him hadn't been working.

Any sexual activity outside God's design is forbidden because it is counterproductive to the process of sanctification. In other words, don't expect to reap the fruit of the Spirit and enjoy fulfillment as a Christian if you are sowing seeds in Satan's kingdom through sexual immorality. Knowing that God's will for our lives is our sanctification (1 Thessalonians 4) is the basis for the following six specific instructions relating to sex.

1. We Are to Abstain from Premarital Sex

It has become common, even expected, in our culture for couples to sleep together and even live together before marriage or in lieu of marriage. They justify their actions by saying, "Love is what counts—who needs a marriage certificate?" or "How can we know if we're sexually compatible unless we sleep together?" The world places a high value on physical attraction and sexual compatibility in finding a partner. Christians are far from immune to this influence. During my early years of ministry, 18 of the first 20 Christian couples I counseled before marriage admitted to me they had slept together—and that was many years ago, from 1972 to 1974.

Fornication is not God's way to seek a life partner. Outward appearance and sexual appeal may attract a person to a potential mate, but neither has the power to hold a couple together. Physical attraction is like perfume or cologne. You smell the fragrance when you put it on, but within minutes your sense of smell is saturated and you barely notice the scent. Similarly, unless you go beyond physical attraction to know and love the real person, the relationship won't last...because there really is no relationship. Sex becomes a selfish animal act instead of an intimate means of expressing love between a male and a female child of God.

Christian dating is not like shopping for a good-looking, comfortable pair of shoes. Shoes get scuffed, worn, and dated, and you have to replace them every year or two. Christian dating is the process of finding God's will for a lifetime marriage partner. Commitment to Christ and godly character far outweigh physical attraction and sex appeal when it comes to marriage.

2. We Are to Abstain from Extramarital Sex

Doug and Katy came to see me because they were having marital problems. In an angry moment, Doug had told his wife she didn't satisfy him sexually like a previous girlfriend had. In tears, Katy told me how hard she tried to be like that other girl, which was impossible for her. The couple left my office without resolution.

Some time later, Doug came home to find Katy sitting on the couch with a pillow on her lap. She asked him if he loved her. He said he did. Katy replied, "Then I'm going to make you pay for what you said about me for the rest of your life!" She pulled his handgun from under the pillow and shot herself to death.

It is normal to be attracted to your mate by his or her appearance, personality, and other qualities. Christian marriage, however, is a commitment to stay faithful "'til death do us part." Once you are married, all comparisons must end. You will likely be introduced to someone who looks better than your spouse, who seems more sensitive and caring, or who may even be more spiritual, but it doesn't matter. Your commitment is to your spouse and no one else. The best-possible-mate contest is over, and you and your spouse have both won!

As Christians, our first commitment is to Christ, which is the most important relationship we have. Your marriage is a picture of that union, and no other relationship must be allowed to deface that image. The pathway to marital happiness and fulfillment is found in loving and serving your spouse, not in looking for someone you think may bring you greater happiness or sexual pleasure.

Many people who end up in extramarital affairs say they are bored with their spouses sexually. They're not bored with their partners, actually—they're bored with sex because they have depersonalized it. When the focus is on self-centered sex and the partner is viewed as a sex object, boredom is likely. When the focus is on nurturing the total relationship and fulfilling the dreams and expectations of your mate, marital life—including sex—remains a fulfilling experience.

3. We Are Not to Violate the Conscience of Our Spouse

A number of years ago I conducted a one-day conference entitled "For Women Only." The participants were invited to ask me questions on any topic. Embarrassing questions were written out and dropped in a basket. Most of the written questions were about sex, and most of those centered on the question, "Must I submit to anything my husband wants me to do sexually?"

If the question is, "Should I submit to anything my husband *needs* sexually?" the answer is yes. According to 1 Corinthians 7:3-5, husbands and wives are not to withhold their bodies from each other:

> The husband should fulfill his marital duty to his wife, and likewise the wife to her husband. The wife's body does not belong to her alone but also to her husband. In the same way, the husband's body

> does not belong to him alone but also to his wife.
> Do not deprive each other except by mutual con-
> sent and for a time, so that you may devote your-
> selves to prayer. Then come together again so that
> Satan will not tempt you because of your lack of
> self-control.

You are not to withhold sex from your spouse or use it as a
weapon against him or her. To do so gives Satan an opportunity
to tempt both of you in areas where you lack self-control.

But should a wife submit to anything her husband *wants* her
to do sexually? No. Neither spouse has the right to violate the
conscience of the other. If a sexual act is morally wrong for one,
it is morally wrong for both. One man protested, "But Scripture
says that the wedding bed is undefiled." I told him to read the
whole verse: "Marriage should be honored by all, and the marriage
bed kept pure, *for God will judge the adulterer and all the sexually
immoral*" (Hebrews 13:4).

Demanding that your spouse violate his or her conscience to
satisfy your lust violates the wedding vow of loving one another
and destroys the intimacy of a relationship built on trust. A
person can and should meet the legitimate sexual needs of his or
her marriage partner. In no way, though, should you demand
that your spouse try to satisfy your lust. In the first place, your
spouse can't. Only Christ can resolve your problem with lust.
The more you feed lustful desires, the more they grow. Second,
it is degrading and demeaning to demand that your spouse perform sexual acts against his or her conscience. Only Christ can
break that cycle of bondage and give you the freedom to love
your spouse as Christ loved the church.

4. We Are to Abstain from Sexual Fantasy

The tempting thought to pull off the freeway and rent a sexually explicit video was overwhelming. Scott was married, with
two children still living at home, but he struggled with sexual

fantasies. As he sped closer to the off-ramp, a conflict raged within him. He knew his actions wouldn't be pleasing to God. He knew he would feel ashamed when it was all over. He knew he would be humiliated if his wife or children came home unexpectedly and found him acting out his fantasy. But he was propelled to the video store like a heroin addict to a fix.

Scott had found many ways to satisfy his secret craving for sexual excitement and release: pornographic paperback novels and magazines, textbooks on the subject of sexuality, sexual fantasies while in the shower, and steamy videos featuring nudity and sex (he avoided the more obvious X-rated films, reasoning that the R-rated ones were easier to explain if he got caught).

He ignored the "way of escape" provided to him by God and took the familiar exit off the freeway. He made his selection in the video shop and headed home for an afternoon of sexual fantasy. After watching the sexually graphic movie, he was flooded with shame and guilt. *How did I get sucked into this pattern again?* he agonized. *Lord, what am I going to do?* He had told no one about his struggle and repeated failures—not his wife, not his pastor, not even the two Christian counselors he had seen in the past for related problems. He felt weak, helpless, and alone. Even God seemed distant and unavailable. So Scott just stuffed his feelings and continued his charade of being the model Christian.

Sexual fantasy plagues many Christian men and women. They may not be physically involved in premarital or extramarital sex, but they have numerous affairs in their minds—an endless variety of sexual adventures with people they know, characters in books, magazines, or video screens, and phantom lovers they dream up on their own. Most sexual fantasy addicts find release in masturbation, which often leads to extramarital affairs.

Sexual fantasy may be regarded by many as harmless self-pleasuring, but Christians are to seek mental purity for at least three different reasons.

First, according to Jesus' words in Matthew 5:27-29, *the seeds for adultery are sown in the heart:*

> You have heard that it was said, "Do not commit adultery." But I tell you that anyone who looks at a woman lustfully has already committed adultery with her in his heart. If your right eye causes you to sin, gouge it out and throw it away. It is better for you to lose one part of your body than for your whole body to be thrown into hell.

Jesus says we should cut off our right hand as well *if* it is neces- sary—but it isn't necessary and that is not where the problem lies. If that were the answer, we would all be cutting off body parts and be bloody torsos rolling down the aisles of our churches...and we still wouldn't have solved the problem.

The passage teaches that looking is the evidence that adultery has already been conceived in the heart. In the same chapter, in verses 21 and 22, Jesus teaches that anyone who is angry with his brother is guilty before the court, and that calling one's brother a name is the same as murder. That would make us all guilty of adultery and murder! We are! In the Sermon on the Mount, Jesus is teaching what genuine righteousness is. It is not merely external conformity to the law, which we can't do anyway. He is teaching that the seeds of murder and adultery are sown in our hearts and minds. It isn't what goes into a person that defiles him, it is what comes out from the seeds that have been sown.

To solve the problem, something has to be done about our heart—and God *has* done something. Ezekiel prophesied that God would give us a new heart and a new spirit (11:19-20; 18:31; 36:26). The heart is the center of our self. Only in the heart do the mind, emotions, and will converge. We can intel- lectually acknowledge the truth, but if it doesn't touch our hearts, it will not change our character. When the truth does penetrate our hearts, our emotions and our will are affected. "Above all else, guard your heart, for it is the wellspring of life"

(Proverbs 4:23). To have victory over sin, we have to win the battle for our mind and keep our heart pure.

Second, according to James 1:14-15, *sexual immorality in the mind precipitates a sexually immoral act:* "Each one is tempted when, by his own evil desire, he is dragged away and enticed. Then, after desire has conceived, it gives birth to sin; and sin, when it is full-grown, gives birth to death." We may think our sexual fantasies will never be acted out, but eventually "out of the overflow of the heart the mouth speaks" (Matthew 12:34). What is sown and nurtured as a seed in the heart will eventually flower as a deed.

Third, *sexual fantasy depersonalizes sex and devalues people.* Sexual fantasy is not a shared marital relationship but a breeding ground for lust and self-gratification that are mushrooming out of control. When sex becomes boring (which it certainly will with the mentality of "all take and no give"), a person will likely look for a more exciting partner.

One man assured me that his sexual fantasizing was not a sin because he visualized girls without heads! I told him, "That's precisely the problem. You have depersonalized sex." This is what pornography does. Sex objects are never properly valued as people created in God's image, much less someone's daughter or son. Treating someone as an object for personal gratification goes against everything the Bible teaches about the dignity and value of human life.

5. We Are to Abstain from Out-of-Control Masturbation

Masturbation is seen by some as a harmless, pleasurable means of releasing sexual pressure. Those who practice, condone, or recommend it say it is a private way of gratifying sexual needs without fear of disease or pregnancy.

The Bible is virtually silent on the topic of masturbation, and Christians have widely divided opinions about it. Some believe it is a God-given means to release pent-up sexual energy when we are unmarried or when our mate is unavailable. In that sense, they believe masturbation can be a means of sexual self-control. At the other extreme are Christians who condemn it as a sin.

Those in favor remind us that it is nowhere condemned in the Bible, that it poses no health risks, and that it may help prevent acts of sexual immorality. Those opposed state that it is sex without a marriage partner and therefore wrong, that it is self-centered, that it is accompanied by sexual fantasies, and that it can lead to an uncontrollable habit.

I certainly don't want to add any restrictions that God doesn't teach, nor do I want to contribute to the legalistic condemnation that is already being heaped on people. But why do so many Christians feel guilty after masturbating? Is it because the church or their parents have said it is wrong, and therefore the guilt is only psychological? If so, the condemnation springs from a conscience that has been developed improperly. The condemnation may also come from the accuser of the brethren (Revelation 12:10).

To consider if masturbation is contributing to your sexual bondage, ask yourself the following questions:

1. Are you committing the mental adultery that Jesus condemned?

2. Are you seeking to put pornographic images in your mind?

3. Has masturbation replaced sexual intimacy in your marriage?

4. Can you stop masturbating? (If you can't, then you have lost some degree of self-control.)

5. Do you sense the Holy Spirit's conviction when you masturbate?

Perhaps you are able to masturbate without depriving your spouse or defiling your mind. Hopefully, you are not chained to the act and can stop at will. If you can't, there is encouraging hope for you if you are trapped in the web of sexual fantasy and out-of-control masturbation. God has provided a way of escape for every temptation.

As you struggle to gain your freedom in Christ, remember that "there is now no condemnation for those who are in Christ Jesus" (Romans 8:1). Guilt and shame do not produce good mental health—but love, acceptance, and affirmation do. God loves you, and He will not give up on you. You may despair in confessing again and again, but His love and forgiveness are unending.

6. We Are to Abstain from Homosexual Behavior

God's view of homosexuality hasn't changed, even though it is politically correct to accept this "alternate lifestyle." The New Testament places homosexuality in the same category as other sexual sins we must avoid:

> Do not be deceived: Neither the sexually immoral nor idolaters nor adulterers nor male prostitutes nor homosexual offenders nor thieves nor the greedy nor drunkards nor slanderers nor swindlers will inherit the kingdom of God (1 Corinthians 6:9-10).

Some argue, "But I was born this way. I have always had homosexual tendencies. I can't help it—this is the way God created me." God did not create anyone to be a homosexual. He created us male and female. Homosexuality is a lie. There is no such thing as a homosexual; there are homosexual *feelings, tendencies,* and *behaviors.* Neither did God create pedophiles, adulterers, or alcoholics. If a person can rationalize homosexual behavior, why can't another rationalize adultery, fornication, pedophilia, and so on?

Because of the fall, we are all genetically predisposed to certain strengths and weaknesses. Some people can become addicted to alcohol faster than others, but that does not make them alcoholics. Rather, they *choose* to drink—in order to party without inhibitions, or cope with life, or stop the pain. Some boys may have lower levels of testosterone and develop more slowly than others, or are raised by overbearing, abusive parents, or are sexually exploited, but that does not make them homosexuals. Coming to terms with our past and the lies we have believed is crucial for our recovery in Christ.

For some sick reason, our culture is bent on finding the ultimate sexual experience without regard for whether it is right or wrong. When we think we've found it, it satisfies for only a season, so the quest must continue. Instead, we should be bent on finding the ultimate personal relationship: "Blessed are those who hunger and thirst for righteousness, for they shall be satisfied" (Matthew 5:6 NASB). Are you willing to pursue the greatest of all relationships, the one that every child of God can have with his heavenly Father? If so, you will be satisfied.

CHAPTER THREE

Reaping the Harvest

*Continence is the only guarantee of an undefiled
spirit, and the best protection against the promiscuity
that cheapens and finally kills the power to love.*

GENE TUNNEY

CONSEQUENCES. What goes up must come down. Every action
has an equal but opposite reaction. If you jump off a tall building
without the benefit of a parachute, hang glider, or bungee cord,
you will drop to the sidewalk like a rock. Plant watermelon
seeds and you will harvest watermelons if you nurture the plant.
Everything we do and every choice we make has consequences.
Cause and effect is built into the universe, and we will reap
what we sow.

If we sow seeds of sexual purity, we will reap the benefits in
marriage. If we sow seeds of sexual immorality, we will reap a
dark harvest of negative personal and spiritual consequences.
"The one who sows to his own flesh will from the flesh reap corruption, but the one who sows to the Spirit will from the Spirit
reap eternal life" (Galatians 6:8 NASB).

What are the consequences of sowing to the flesh in reference
to sexual conduct? What kind of corruption is Paul talking
about? First, there are the obvious outward or physical and

relational consequences, which we will deal with in this chapter. Second, there are the inward or spiritual consequences, which we will explore in the next chapter.

The Harvest Experienced in Body and in Marriage

The most obvious consequences of ignoring God's design for sex and marriage are the physical and relational consequences. Physical pain, the threat of disease and death, and the breakup of a relationship are quickly noticed and felt. Consider the AIDS epidemic. If the trend continues, 70 million people will die from this disease in the next generation. It is the most incurable disease plaguing humanity, but it is also the most preventable. All you have to do is abstain.

Free sex isn't free, and those who pursue it aren't living in freedom. Sexual promiscuity leads to disgusting forms of bondage, and the potential price tag in terms of health alone is staggering.

A report from the Centers for Disease Control from the year 2000 tells us that

> in the United States, more than 65 million people are currently living with an incurable sexually transmitted disease (STD). An additional 15 million people become infected with one or more STDs each year, roughly half of whom contract lifelong infections (Cates, 1999).

If the prediction of new infections is correct, then more than 60 million additional people contracted an STD in the period from 1999 to 2004. Further, STDs "add billions of dollars to the nation's healthcare costs each year" and "are difficult to track. Many people with these infections do not have symptoms and remain undiagnosed…These 'hidden' epidemics are magnified with each new infection that goes unrecognized and untreated."[2]

Medical health experts insist that STDs are by far the most prevalent of communicable diseases. The problem is no longer epidemic, but pandemic.

The most frightening aspect of STDs is that they can be passed on without the carrier exhibiting any symptoms. This is especially true for those who test positive for HIV. Victims may go for years without showing signs of illness, unknowingly passing on the disease to their sexual partners, who in turn pass it on to other unsuspecting victims. Without medical testing, people cannot be sure that their sexual partners are free of all STDs. Indeed, partners may not even know they are infected. The rapid spread of STDs in our culture illustrates the chilling truth that a sexual encounter involves more than two people. If you have sex with a promiscuous person, as far as STDs are concerned, you are also having sex with every one of that person's previous sex partners, and you are vulnerable to the diseases carried by all of them.

People who have violated God's design for sex also pay a price in their marriage relationships. Those who have had unholy sex don't seem to enjoy holy sex. I have counseled many women who can't stand to be touched by their husbands because of past sexual experiences. Incredibly, their feelings change almost immediately after finding their freedom in Christ from sexual bondages. One pastor had been snubbed sexually by his wife for ten years because of bondage that had blocked her from sexual intimacy. To their mutual surprise, the couple was able to come together sexually after she found her freedom in Christ.

Promiscuity before marriage leads to lack of sexual fulfillment in marriage. The euphoria that comes from sex outside God's will quickly dissipates and leaves the participant in bondage to sin. If the past sexual sins were consensual, the bondages only increase as the individual attempts to satisfy his or her lust, which can't be satisfied. The more lustful habits are fed, the faster they grow. If the sins were not consensual, meaning that the person went along with the act but didn't want to or was forced to, then he or she is not able to enjoy wholesome marital relations until the past is resolved. Such people lack the freedom to enjoy mutual expressions of love and trust.

If people have been victims of severe sexual abuse such as rape or incest, their bodies have been used unwillingly as instruments of unrighteousness. Tragically, these victims have become one flesh with their abusers and have great difficulty relating to their spouses in a healthy way. It's not fair that these people were violated against their will. It's sick, and the sickness pollutes what should be a beautiful and fulfilling marriage relationship. The good news is that people can be set free from the bondage caused by such violations. They can renounce the unrighteous uses of their body, submit to God, resist the devil, and forgive those who abused them.

The Defilement of a Family

One of the most heartrending consequences of sexual sin is the effect it has on the children of the offender. The affair between King David of Israel and Bathsheba, wife of Uriah the Hittite, illustrates the downward spiral of personal defilement and its effect on the family. Even though David is called a man after God's own heart (Acts 13:22), he had a dark blot on his life. First Kings 15:5 summarizes his life: "David had done what was right in the eyes of the LORD and had not failed to keep any of the LORD's commands all the days of his life—except in the case of Uriah the Hittite." Because of his moral failure, David's family paid a steep price. Let's consider his steps to defilement and their tragic consequences.

"One evening David got up from his bed and walked around on the roof of the palace. From the roof he saw a woman bathing. The woman was very beautiful, and David sent someone to find out about her" (2 Samuel 11:2-3). There was nothing wrong with the woman, Bathsheba, being beautiful, and there was nothing wrong with David being attracted to her.

That's the way God made us. Bathsheba may have been wrong for bathing where others could see her, and David was definitely wrong for continuing to look at her. For such occasions, God provides a way of escape. David could have turned and walked away from the tempting sight, but he didn't.

When David sent messengers to get Bathsheba, he was far down the path of defilement—making the possibility of stopping more difficult with each step. The two slept together, and she became pregnant. David tried to cover up his sin by calling Uriah, Bathsheba's husband, home from the battlefield, in the expectation that he would sleep with her. The pregnancy could then have been attributed to him, but the noble Uriah wouldn't cooperate. He didn't want to have any privileges his men didn't have. So David sent him back to the battlefield and arranged for him to be killed. Now David the adulterer was also David the murderer! Sin has a way of compounding itself. If you think living righteously is hard, try living unrighteously. Cover-up, denial, and guilt make for a very complex life.

After a period of mourning her dead husband, Bathsheba became David's wife. David suffered physical consequences because of his guilt and shame. In Psalm 32:3 he describes his torment: "When I kept silent, my bones wasted away through my groaning all day long. For day and night your hand was heavy upon me; my strength was sapped as in the heat of summer."

The Lord allowed plenty of time for David to acknowledge his sin. The king didn't confess, so God sent the prophet Nathan to confront him. God won't let His children live in darkness for long because He knows it will eat them alive. One pastor with a pornography addiction traveled to a pastors' conference. His colleagues asked for copies of his ministry materials, and when the pastor opened his briefcase with a crowd around him, he suddenly realized he had brought the wrong case. His stack of smutty magazines was there for all to see! "How embarrassing!" or "How tragic!" you say. On the contrary, the exposure caused him to seek the help he needed. "There is nothing concealed that will not be disclosed, or hidden that will not be made known" (Matthew 10:26).

Sadly, the public lives of many Christians are radically different from their private lives. As long as they think the facade can continue, they will likely not deal with their own issues. Ironically, these people are often the ones who are most critical of others. People who haven't dealt with their own guilt and shame often seek to "balance their internal scales" by projecting guilt and blame on others. The Lord says in Matthew 7:1-5,

> Do not judge, or you too will be judged. For in the same way you judge others, you will be judged, and with the measure you use, it will be measured to you.
>
> Why do you look at the speck of sawdust in your brother's eye and pay no attention to the plank in your own eye? How can you say to your brother, "Let me take the speck out of your eye," when all the time there is a plank in your own eye? You hypocrite, first take the plank out of your own eye, and then you will see clearly to remove the speck from your brother's eye.

Forgiveness and Consequences

David finally acknowledged his sins, both of which were capital offenses under the law. Then Nathan declared, "The LORD has taken away your sin. You are not going to die. But because by doing this you have made the enemies of the LORD show utter contempt, the son born to you will die" (2 Samuel 12:13-14).

The enemies of the Lord are Satan and his angels. I don't think the average sinning Christian has a clue concerning the moral outrage his or her sexual sins cause in the spiritual realm. Satan, the accuser of the brethren, throws them into God's face day and night (Revelation 12:10). Our private, secret sins are committed openly before the god of this world and his fallen angelic horde! Far worse, our sexual sins are an offense to God, who is grieved by our failure and who must endure the utter contempt of Satan. Besides, our hypocrisy is known by the world and our witness is compromised.

The Lord spared David, but his and Bathsheba's son died. Why did he have to die? It is possible that God had to cut off the rebellious seed sown by David so that the male offspring of this adulterous relationship did not receive the birthright! We are talking about the throne of David upon which the Messiah would reign. God took the infant home to be with Himself, and David had the assurance that he would be with the child in eternity (2 Samuel 12:23).

Additional judgment was meted out to David's household as a result of his sin. The prophet Nathan further declared,

> This is what the LORD says: "Out of your own household I am going to bring calamity upon you. Before your very eyes I will take your wives and give them to one who is close to you, and he will lie with your wives in broad daylight. You did it in secret, but I will do this thing in broad daylight before Israel" (2 Samuel 12:11).

The Lord's word was fulfilled when Absalom, one of David's sons, "lay with his father's concubines in the sight of all Israel" (2 Samuel 16:22).

Amnon, another son of David, followed his father's example to an even more despicable level of sexual immorality (2 Samuel 13). His lust for his virgin half sister Tamar, Absalom's sister, provoked him to play on her sympathies with a feigned illness. When Tamar came to his room to take care of him, Amnon tried to seduce her. When she refused his advances, he raped her. Apparently Amnon could have gone through legitimate channels to take Tamar as his wife. But his lust demanded to be satisfied *now*.

Great calamity came upon David as a result of his sin. In all, four of his sons died prematurely: Bathsheba's son died at birth, Amnon was killed by his brother Absalom in retaliation for the rape of Tamar, and Absalom and Adonijah were both killed attempting to take the throne from their father. All this came upon David because he failed to turn away from the tempting sight of a woman bathing. It is critical for us and for our loved ones to take every thought captive to the obedience of Christ (2 Corinthians 10:5).

Nature or Nurture...or Is It Spiritual?

In the Ten Commandments, God said

> You shall not make for yourself an idol, or any likeness of what is in heaven above or on the earth beneath or in the water under the earth. You shall not worship them or serve them; for I, the LORD your God, am a jealous God, visiting the iniquity of the fathers on the children, on the third and the fourth generations of those who hate Me, but showing lovingkindness to thousands, to those who love Me and keep My commandments (Exodus 20:4-6 NASB; see also Deuteronomy 5:9-10; Exodus 34:6-7; Deuteronomy 7:9-10; and Numbers 14:18).

This affirms that God blesses those who are obedient to His covenant to the thousandth generation, but that the iniquities of those who are disobedient are passed on to the third and fourth generations.

How does this work? Anybody working with hurting people knows that the abusers have been abused themselves. The cycle of abuse is a well-attested social phenomenon. Do we inherit a specific bent toward sin from our parents—and if we do, is this transmission genetic (nature), environmental (nurture), or spiritual? I believe the correct answers are *yes* and *all three!* First, there is plenty of evidence to show we are genetically predisposed to certain strengths and weaknesses. However, we cannot blame genetics for our own bad choices.

Second, environmental factors definitely contribute to sinful behavior being passed on from one generation to the next. For example, if you were raised in a home where pornography was readily available and sexual promiscuity was modeled, you would certainly be influenced in this direction. Unless parents deal with their sins, they unwittingly set up the next generation to repeat their moral failures. "A student is not above his teacher, but everyone who is fully trained will be like his teacher" (Luke 6:40).

Third, there seems to be an inherited spiritual bent toward sin as well. For instance, Abraham lied about his wife, calling her his sister. Later his son Isaac did exactly the same thing. Then Isaac's son Jacob lied in order to steal his brother's birthright, and told many other lies as well. This is a spiritual phenomenon. Nobody is suggesting that Abraham said to Isaac, "Listen, son, if you ever get in a jam, just pass your wife off as your sister. It didn't work for me, but maybe it will for you."

How It Happens

In the Old Testament, the Israelites confessed their sins and iniquities and those of their ancestors. Iniquities relate more to a rebellious spirit or strong will. Somehow these iniquities are passed on from one generation to another. Old Testament scholar S.J. De Vries explains this:

> In its early development Israel was very much influenced by a dynamic concept of corporate sin... The family group was a much more significant entity than the individual person. When the head of such a group transgressed, he transmitted guilt to every member of it...Thus, according to the Decalogue [Ten Commandments]...the iniquity of the father is to be visited upon the children.[3]

Speaking about idolatry, Hosea mentions demonic spirits affecting children, which is related to the parents' sins:

> They consult a wooden idol and are answered by a stick of wood. A spirit of prostitution leads them astray; they are unfaithful to their God. They sacrifice on the mountaintops and burn offerings on the hills, under oak, poplar and terebinth, where the shade is pleasant. Therefore your daughters turn to prostitution and your daughters-in-law to adultery (Hosea 4:12-13).

The cause of the children's sexual sins is not only the parents' sin of idolatry, but also the demonic "spirit of prostitution."

How did the Israelites deal with ancestral sins? Here are some examples:

> Those of Israelite descent had separated themselves from all foreigners. They stood in their places and confessed their sins and the wickedness of their fathers (Nehemiah 9:2).

> I confess the sins we Israelites, including myself and my father's house, have committed against you (Nehemiah 1:6).

> O LORD, we acknowledge our wickedness and the guilt of our fathers; we have indeed sinned against you (Jeremiah 14:20).

> We have not obeyed the LORD our God or kept the laws he gave us through his servants the prophets. All Israel transgressed your law and turned away, refusing to obey you.

> Therefore the curses and sworn judgments written in the Law of Moses, the servant of God, have been poured out on us, because we have sinned against you (Daniel 9:10-11).

God had spoken, and the prophets had warned the people about generational sins. However, in the early sixth century B.C., the prophet Ezekiel had to correct an abuse:

> The word of the LORD came to me: "What do you people mean by quoting this proverb about the land of Israel: 'The fathers eat sour grapes, and the children's teeth are set on edge?' As surely as I live, declares the Sovereign LORD, you will no longer quote this proverb in Israel" (Ezekiel 18:1-3).

This popular Israelite proverb was not from the book of Proverbs, nor was it from the mouth of God. The problem Ezekiel was trying to correct was a fatalistic response to the law and the abdication of personal responsibility. Children are not guilty because of their parents' sins and they will not be punished for their parents' iniquities, which are visited upon them, if they are diligent to turn away from the sins of their parents. Ezekiel (see also Jeremiah 31:29-30)

> did not mean to deny corporate sin: this was beyond dispute. [His] purpose was to accentuate individual responsibility, which was in danger of becoming submerged in a consciousness of overpowering national calamity. Even though the nation was now suffering a bitter corporate punishment, there was hope for the individual if he would repent.[4]

Sowing Seeds of Repentance

We have seen in the Old Testament the transmission of sin from one generation to the next, and how the prophets called the people to confess their sins and the sins of their fathers. An unholy inheritance cannot be dealt with passively. We must consciously take our place in Christ and renounce the sins of our ancestors. We are not guilty of our parents' sins, but because they sinned, their sins may be passed on to us. That is why we are told in Leviticus 26:40 to confess our own sin and the sin of our forefathers "in their unfaithfulness which they committed against Me, and also in their acting with hostility against Me" (NASB). The opposite is to cover up and defend the sins of our parents, grandparents, and others, and continue in the cycle of bondage.

The possibility of overcoming generational sins is evidenced in the life of Joseph, one of Jacob's sons. Joseph chose not to follow in the ways of his father, grandfather, and great-grandfather, even though he was given every opportunity to lie to protect himself from his jealous brothers. In fact, the more he told the truth, the more trouble he endured. If he was predisposed to lying, he chose not to comply. Eventually he was totally vindicated for his honesty.

I frequently minister to people who repeat the sins of their parents and grandparents. Are they forced to do these things? No! But they will repeat them if they continue to hold iniquity in their hearts, which can be visited to the third and fourth generations.

Under the Old Covenant, as we saw, all of God's chosen people were called to repent of their sins and iniquities regardless of whether the scope of their offenses was personal or national. National or corporate repentance cannot happen without individual repentance. This is not just an Old Testament concept. Paul wrote, "Just as sin entered the world through one man, and death through sin, and in this way death came to all men, because all have sinned…" (Romans 5:12). Peter wrote that we have been redeemed from our "futile way of life inherited from [our] forefathers" (1 Peter 1:18 NASB).

No matter what our ancestors have done, if we repent and believe in Christ, God rescues us from the dominion of darkness and brings us into the kingdom of His dear Son (Colossians 1:13). We are under a new covenant, which promises, "Their sins and lawless acts I will remember no more" (Hebrews 10:17).

Repentance Breaks the Chain

Repentance is God's answer to sin and iniquity. Truth sets us free, but we won't experience that freedom without repentance. Repentance literally means "a change of mind," but it isn't genuine unless we have turned away from our sins and iniquities and turned toward God and the truth. Members of the early church began their public profession of faith by literally facing the west and declaring, "I renounce you, Satan, and all your works and ways." Then they would face the east and proclaim their faith in God. In so doing, they reclaimed any ground they or their forefathers had given to Satan. (How to experience our freedom through repentance will be discussed in later chapters.)

It is important to understand that God has forgiven us even before we repent, but He doesn't necessarily take away the natural consequences of our sin. If He did, it wouldn't take us long to figure out that we could sin all we want and then turn to God for cleansing without any repercussions. If you have contracted an STD, you will still have it after you have fully repented.

It is also important to realize that when parents repent there is no guarantee that their children will. Even if they were influenced genetically, environmentally, or spiritually in the direction of your sin, your children are still responsible for their own choices. They may choose to repeat or not to repeat your failures, as well as your successes. Have you ever noticed that bad health is contagious, but good health isn't? Paul wrote, "Do not be misled: 'Bad company corrupts good character'" (1 Corinthians 15:33). Your children may have "caught" your bad habits from you, but they won't necessarily catch repentance from you. However, your repentant, healthy, God-fearing lifestyle will hopefully influence them to make their own choice to renounce sin and trust Christ.

An Example to Follow

David's sexual sin and murderous cover-up was tragic, and the consequences of sin in his own life and in the lives of his children were painful and long-lasting. However, David's own personal story has a good ending. He responded to his sin correctly and went on to shepherd Israel with integrity of heart and lead them with skillful hands (Psalm 78:72). His seed-line provided the human link for the Satan-crushing soul-Redeemer promised in Genesis 3:15.

David's confession of sin in Psalm 51 is a model prayer for those who violate God's plan for sexual purity:

> Have mercy on me, O God, according to your unfailing love; according to your great compassion blot out my transgressions. Wash away all my iniquity and cleanse me from my sin.
>
> For I know my transgressions, and my sin is always before me. Against you, you only, have I sinned and done what is evil in your sight, so that you are proved right when you speak and justified when you judge...
>
> Create in me a pure heart, O God, and renew a steadfast spirit within me. Do not cast me from your presence or take your Holy Spirit from me. Restore to me the joy of your salvation and grant me a willing spirit, to sustain me (verses 1-4,10-12).

There is one major difference, however. David related to God under the Old Covenant, but we have the privilege of relating to God under the New Covenant. Under the covenant grace of God, we are forgiven, and He will *never* leave us or forsake us. He has also given us a new heart and a new spirit. With God's love and presence in our lives, we can be guaranteed the outcome of this war because the battle has already been won.

So don't be discouraged with the sobering reality of the natural consequences of sinful choices. God loves you because God is love. It is His nature to love you, and that is why His love is unconditional. Life without Christ is a hopeless end, but life with Christ is an endless hope. Be encouraged—Jesus Christ has broken the power of sin, defeated the devil, given you a new life in Him, and set you free. You may not feel free right now, but keep reading, and don't stop until you finish the last chapter.

CHAPTER FOUR

The Addiction Cycle

*Some psychological and sociological conditioning
occurs in every person's life and this affects
the decisions they make. But we must resist the
modern concept that all sin can be explained
merely on the basis of conditioning.*

FRANCIS SCHAEFFER

BEING A CLUB DIRECTOR WITH YOUTH FOR CHRIST was my first
official ministry. On the night I was talking about sex, a young man
came with his girlfriend. At the end of my talk he asked, "I am not
a Christian, but if I had sex with my girlfriend, would either of us
regret it later?" That is the most mature question I have ever
heard from a teenager. If only everybody would consider the
consequences of their choices, and then make the right decision.

We know that David regretted his sinful choice to have sex
with Bathsheba. Let's look further into the story of his son
Amnon and see how he deteriorated into raping his half sister
Tamar. As with David, it began in innocent infatuation but pro-
gressed to mental obsession. "Amnon son of David fell in love
with Tamar...Amnon became frustrated to the point of illness on
account of his sister Tamar, for she was a virgin, and it seemed
impossible for him to do anything to her" (2 Samuel 13:1,2).

What Amnon called love was really lust, as evidenced by his selfish behavior.

Solomon warned in Proverbs 6:25-26, "Do not lust in your heart after her beauty or let her captivate you with her eyes, for the prostitute reduces you to a loaf of bread, and the adulteress preys upon your very life." Tamar was not a prostitute, but the sexual fantasy in Amnon's mind had been replayed so many times that he was physically sick. He had looked lustfully once too often. The opportunity to find the way of escape was gone. The affair in his mind had been played over many times. Lust fueled by sexual fantasy screams for expression. So Amnon and his friend Jonadab concocted a plan to get Tamar into Amnon's bed.

Once a plan to fulfill the demands of lust is set in motion, it is seldom stopped. Amnon had lost control, and where there is no self-control, all reason is gone. Amnon's lust had reduced him to a "loaf of bread." He was "like one of the wicked fools in Israel" (2 Samuel 13:13).

Ironically, right after his violation of Tamar, "Amnon hated her with intense hatred. In fact, he hated her more than he had loved her. Amnon said to her, 'Get up and get out!'"(2 Samuel 13:15). Amnon didn't love Tamar. He never once considered what was best for her. He was trapped in a cycle of sexual addiction. People living in bondage hate that which controls them. Alcoholics crave a drink, but when they have had their fill, they smash the bottle against the wall in remorse, only to buy another bottle when the craving returns. The pornography addict burns his magazines, tosses his X-rated videos into the garbage, and tells his lover he never wants to see her again. But when the lust fires rekindle—as they always do—he's back to his old haunts, looking for a sexual fix. The downward spiral of sexual degradation is predictable.

The Addiction Cycle

The addiction cycle is basically the same for every form of bondage. The cycle begins with a baseline experience. It represents who we are and what we are experiencing at the time of our first exposure to sex, drugs, or alcohol.

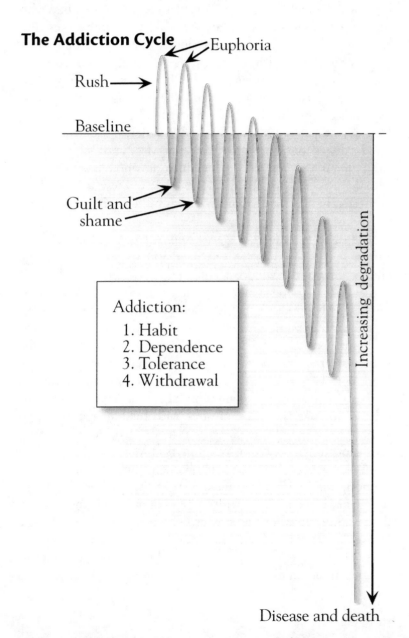

The Addiction Cycle

Euphoria

Rush→

Baseline

Guilt and shame

Addiction:
1. Habit
2. Dependence
3. Tolerance
4. Withdrawal

Increasing degradation

Disease and death

There is an emotional–physical rush when we are stimulated by some sexual thought or experience—ending in a euphoric high, which quickly declines. Consider Joe, a teenaged boy, who notices a new girl in class. Mary is a real beauty in his eyes, and he feels a rush of emotion just looking at her. When Mary returns his glance with a smile, Joe's face flushes and his heart races with excitement. He's never felt so good. When the bell rings and Mary walks out of class, Joe returns to his baseline experience. The rush is over for now...but he liked what he felt. He can't wait to see Mary again and experience the rush.

For weeks Joe steals little glances at Mary and feels his heart throb. Joe is a normal boy and a Christian who has standards of sexual purity. He initially has Mary's best interest at heart. The attraction he has for her wins out over his fear of rejection, and he invites her out for a date.

Riding in the car with Mary brings the rush to new heights. When she innocently reaches over and touches his leg, Joe almost flies out the window! They hold hands and end the date with a light hug. Joe is in love. So far, so good. He has not compromised his standards, but he begins to imagine what it might feel like if they went a little further.

Before long a hug and then a kiss from Mary don't give Joe the same rush they first did. To have the same euphoric experience, Joe has to become a little more adventurous. However, going further means he has to compromise his moral convictions just a little. Joe has become more free with his hands during passionate good-night kisses. When he's alone he begins to fantasize about touching and kissing other parts of Mary's body.

At first stepping over the line brought him immediate gratification, and it was pleasurable. But as the euphoria declines, Joe's conscience kicks in with twinges of guilt and shame. The flesh, however, wants to go further. Every new compromise brings greater conviction, which is followed by greater compromise. He discovers that a drink or fix helps him overcome his inhibitions and dulls his conscience. Joe—and perhaps Mary as well—is on a downward-spiraling addictive cycle. He can stop, but does he want to?

Result: Bondage

The euphoric experiences of sexual and chemical highs wear off, and more stimulation is needed to get that same high. Every successive use or experience increases our tolerance to sex and chemicals. As lust grows, more stimulation is required to quench it. But it can't be satisfied. The more a fleshly desire is fed, the larger it grows. Normal sexual experiences don't seem to bring the euphoria that a simple touch once did. So other sexual experiences must be tried to get that same high. We just want to have the first initial rush that felt so good, but greater levels of degradation take us further away, and our lifestyle has also moved far away from our baseline experience. Self-gratification dominates our thinking, and we have long since stopped considering the other person more important than ourselves (see Philippians 2:1-5). When we violate another person's conscience or moral boundaries, we have quenched the Spirit.

As the decline continues, a sexual habit brings an increasing dependence on the experience. The euphoria becomes a means of releasing stress and tension. The mind is filled with pornographic images and the memory of actual experiences. Many people in sexual bondage begin to withdraw from others and from God as the degradation continues. The unchecked cycle of sexual addiction opens the door to sexually transmitted diseases and death for some. Those addicts with a strong conscience against violating others turn to self-gratification, and pornography and uncontrolled masturbation dominate their private world.

In a godly Christian marriage, love and trust are the means for having sexual intimacy, which can be extremely pleasurable for a husband and wife who love each other. For those who are sexually addicted, though, fear and danger replace love and trust. A married man shared that he filled his craving for "exciting" sex by carrying on an adulterous affair in a motel. He and his "lover" liked to perform sex with the curtains open or late at night in the motel swimming pool. For this man, sex with his Christian wife had become unexciting because his lust was reinforced by fear and danger.

Spiritual Degeneration Brings Physical Degradation

The shameful decline of sexual addiction is depicted in Romans 1:24-28:

> God gave them over in the sinful desires of their hearts to sexual impurity for the degrading of their bodies with one another. They exchanged the truth of God for a lie, and worshiped and served the created things rather than the Creator—who is forever praised. Amen.
>
> Because of this, God gave them over to shameful lusts. Even their women exchanged natural relations for unnatural ones. In the same way the men also abandoned natural relations with women and were inflamed with lust for one another. Men committed indecent acts with other men, and received in themselves the due penalty for their perversion.
>
> Furthermore, since they did not think it worthwhile to retain the knowledge of God, he gave them over to a depraved mind, to do what ought not to be done.

Notice the progression: from shameful lusts to homosexuality to a depraved mind. As a nation, America is probably between stages two and three. Homosexuality is accepted as an alternative lifestyle and protected by our courts. Our minds are becoming increasingly depraved. The frightening thing is that a depraved mind is devoid of logic. It can no longer reason morally, and so we are sliding completely off our moral foundation as a nation.

If you find yourself in this downward spiral personally, realize that your degradation began when you exchanged the truth of God for a lie and began worshiping created things rather than the Creator. In a moment of temptation, you chose to follow lustful desires instead of God's plan for moral purity. With every repeated negative choice, the lie became more deeply entrenched. Satan, the "father of lies" (John 8:44), is winning the battle for your mind.

There are many ways in which we are tempted to exchange the natural for the unnatural in the area of sexual behavior. One is the fascination with oral and anal sex. Before the so-called sexual revolution of the 1960s, those acts were considered sodomy in almost every state in the Union. Even today the media uses the term *sodomy* when referring to oral sex. Young people are experimenting with oral sex because they consider it "safe"—that is, they can't get pregnant. But it's not safe or healthy when sexually transmitted diseases are rampant. To show how far we have come since even the 1960s, in 2003 the United States Supreme Court struck down a Texas law against sodomy and essentially said no state can regulate sexual standards for consenting adults. Today, teenagers don't consider oral sex as "having sex." Whatever they may think, they are still uniting themselves with each other, and outside of marriage, this kind of union brings bondage.

Are oral and anal sex natural? Is that how God designed those body parts to be used? Was one person created to walk on his hands and another on his feet? From the standpoint of hygiene, is it natural to put the mouth so close to orifices designed for the elimination of bodily wastes? This aspect of the sexual revolution has helped homosexuality to proliferate because you don't need the opposite sex to perform oral or anal sex. Have we exchanged the truth of God for a lie? On the other hand, if a Christian couple mutually agrees that oral sex is a natural use of their bodies and that they are not violating each other's conscience, so be it.

Ignorance of the truth is no excuse. Paul clearly warned us that "the wrath of God is revealed from heaven against all ungodliness and unrighteousness of men who suppress the truth in unrighteousness, because that which is known about God is evident within them; for God made it evident" (Romans 1:18-20 NASB). Every conscious choice against the truth numbs the soul's awareness of it. Behaviors once seen as unnatural and indecent are passionately accepted as normal. The conscience becomes seared, and the awareness of God is dimmed.

God gives those who don't honor Him over to degrading passions. When the church at Corinth condoned an incident of sexual perversion, Paul instructed them, "Hand this man over to Satan, so that the flesh may be destroyed and his spirit saved on the day of the Lord" (1 Corinthians 5:5).

Throughout this degenerative process, God graciously offers a way back through Christ. No matter where people may be in their flight from light into darkness, there is a safe passage home. The serial rapists and murderers on death row can throw themselves on the mercy of God and receive His forgiveness. In God's economy, sin is not measured by quality or quantity. Jesus died once for *all* our sins.

Is there hope for those who haven't gone too far? Can we repent of our sinful ways and return to God? Of course we can, and freedom from sexual bondage is possible for every child of God who is willing to submit to God and resist the devil. We can have victory over sin if we understand and appropriate our position in Christ.

Mental Strongholds

When you first came to Christ, hopefully you learned you were a new creation "in Christ," and that old things had passed away. Not only that, you were transferred out of the kingdom of darkness into the kingdom of God's dear Son, and you are no longer "in Adam"—you are alive "in Christ." All that being true, you have probably wondered why you still struggle with some of the same old thoughts and habits. Or maybe you came to Christ hoping that your sexual or chemical addiction would be resolved, but you still have the same cravings and thoughts. There is a logical and biblical explanation as to why that is so.

We were all born physically alive but spiritually dead (Ephesians 2:1). We had neither the presence of God in our lives nor the knowledge of His ways. So during those early and formative years, we all learned how to live our lives independently of God. Then one day we came to Christ, and everything I wrote in the previous paragraph became true of us—but nobody pushed the "clear" button in our mind. Everything that had previously been programmed into our memories was still there. That is why Paul wrote, "Do not conform any longer to the pattern of this world, but be transformed by the renewing of your mind. Then you will be able to test and approve what God's will is—his good, pleasing and perfect will" (Romans 12:2).

Without Christ, we learned how to cope or defend ourselves as a means of survival. Psychologists call these survival means *defense mechanisms*: denial, rationalization, projection, blaming, lying, emotional insulation, and so on. They are similar to what others call *flesh patterns* or *mental strongholds*. These mental habit patterns of thought are habitual pathways grooved into our brains, as with a truck that drives the same route through a pasture every day for months. Deep ruts are formed, and the truck will just stay in the ruts without being steered. In fact, any attempt to steer out of the ruts is met with resistance.

Mental strongholds are assimilated into our mind from the environment in which we are raised in two ways. First, they are primarily developed in mind through our *prevailing experiences,* such as the homes we were raised in, the schools we attended, the churches we went to (or didn't go to), and the friends and enemies we encountered. Mental attitudes are more caught than formally taught. For example, neighborhood friends could have shown you pornographic magazines or experimented with you sexually. Babysitters could have fondled you sexually. Such experiences will have lasting effects on you unless they are dealt with.

Environment isn't the only determinant of mental strongholds, because we each have individual choice. Two children can be raised in the same home by the same parents, eat the same food, play with the same friends, and attend the same church—yet respond differently to life. We are individually created expressions of God's workmanship (Psalm 139:13-14; Ephesians 2:10). Despite similarities in genes and upbringing, our unique personalities and our capacity to make personal choices result in different evaluations of and responses to life.

The second major contributor to the development of strongholds in our mind is *traumatic experiences*. Whereas prevailing experiences are assimilated by our mind over time, traumatic experiences are burned into our memory because of their intensity—for example, the death of a parent, a divorce, incest, or rape. These experiences are stored in our memory bank and influence our thinking. We are not so much in bondage to these experiences as we are in bondage to the lies we choose to believe about God, ourself, and life in general because of the trauma.

As we struggle to reprogram our minds from the negative input of past experiences, we are also confronted daily with an ungodly world system. It is important to realize that we can continue to be conformed to this world, even as Christians, by believing lies, reading wrong material, and so on. We are not immune to worldly influences; we can allow them to affect our thinking and behavior. "See to it that no one takes you captive through hollow and deceptive philosophy, which depends on human tradition and the basic principles of this world rather than on Christ" (Colossians 2:8).

Strongholds and Temptation

Since we live in this world, we will continuously face the temptation to conform to it. It is not a sin to be tempted, however. If it were, Christ would be the worst sinner who ever lived because He was "tempted in every way, just as we are" (Hebrews 4:15). Rather, we sin when we consciously choose to give in to temptation, which Christ never did.

All temptation is an attempt by Satan to get us to live our lives independently of God, to walk according to the flesh rather than according to the Spirit (see Galatians 5:16-23). Satan knows exactly which buttons to push when tempting us because he's a great observer. He knows your weaknesses and your family history. He's aware of the prevailing experiences and traumatic experiences which have made you vulnerable to certain temptations. Based on your past behavior, he knows your vulnerability to sexual temptations.

Each temptation begins with a seed thought placed in our mind by the world, the flesh, or the devil himself.

Some Typical Flesh Patterns

If we continue to act on wrong choices in response to temptation, a habit can be formed in about six weeks. If the habit persists, a stronghold will be developed in the mind.

We are constantly bombarded with sexually stimulating thoughts since sex is used in the media for "entertainment" and to sell everything from beer to cars. Of course, pornography and illicit sexual activities reinforce and strengthen sexual strongholds, but many people don't even need the external world to fantasize because they have programmed so much junk into their minds through the Internet, television, movies, books, and magazines. That's why sexual strongholds are difficult to overcome. Once images are formulated in the mind, the mental pictures are there for instant recall. An alcoholic can't get drunk by fantasizing about a bottle. A drug addict can't get high by imagining himself snorting cocaine. But sexaholics can carry on affairs in their minds and act them out in the privacy of their homes.

An inferiority complex is a major stronghold that many Christians struggle with. We aren't born with an inferiority complex. It comes from living in a competitive world where we compare ourself with someone who runs faster, thinks smarter, or looks prettier. If you are plagued by feelings of inferiority, chances are you were raised in a competitive atmosphere or you chose to compare yourself with others. No matter how hard you tried, you couldn't please your parents or teachers, and someone always outdid you. Your efforts were never quite good enough.

As a redeemed child of God, you now understand that you are inferior to no other person. But deeply ingrained thoughts and feelings from the past seem to drown out the love and affirmation you get from God. You feel trapped on a dead-end street, constantly searching for the acceptance that eluded you as a child. That's a stronghold—and it can only be torn down in Christ.

Consider the variety of strongholds that come from being raised in a home where the father is addicted to alcohol. He comes home drunk and abusive every night. His oldest son is strong enough to stand up to him. There is no way he's going to take anything from this drunk. The middle son doesn't think he can stand up to Dad, so he accommodates him. The youngest son is terrorized. When Dad comes home, he heads for the closet or hides under the bed.

Twenty years later, the father is gone and these three boys are now adults. When they are confronted with a hostile situation, how do you think they respond? The oldest one fights, the middle one accommodates, and the youngest one runs and hides.

A Sexual Stronghold

Homosexuality is a stronghold. Condemning those who struggle with this behavior, however, will prove counterproductive. They don't need any more condemnation. They suffer from an incredible identity crisis already. Overbearing authoritarianism is what has driven many to this lifestyle in the first place.

Most of those who struggle with homosexual tendencies or behaviors have had poor developmental upbringing. Sexual abuse, dysfunctional families (often where the roles of mother and father are reversed), exposure to homosexual literature before they had an opportunity to fully develop their own sexual identity, playground teasing, and poor relationships with the opposite sex have all contributed to their mental and emotional development. Mixed messages lead to mixed emotions.

Charles, a 52-year-old pastor, admitted to me that he had struggled with homosexual tendencies for as long as he could remember. More than once he had given in to those urges. He had begged God to forgive him and take the feelings away. He had attended healing services and self-help groups for those with sexual bondages. Nothing had worked. To his credit, Charles had never once given up on God. He was married and had somehow kept his struggle a secret from his children. (Most people in sexual bondage struggle privately. It is an extremely lonely battle.)

I asked Charles what his earliest childhood memory was. He went back to the age of two. His birth father had left before he was born, and his Christian mother raised him. She had a boyfriend, who occasionally came over and spent the night. On those nights, Charles had to share a bed with this man. His earliest childhood memory was of this man, whom he admired so much, turning his back to him and going to sleep. The little boy was desperately looking for affirmation from a male figure—wanting so much to be loved, accepted, and appreciated.

As I walked him through the Steps to Freedom in Christ, Charles broke down and cried. He forgave his birth father for abandoning him, and he forgave the man who had slept in his bed for rejecting him. Then he renounced every sexual use of his body as an instrument of unrighteousness and gave himself and

his body to the Lord. I also encouraged him to renounce the lie
that he was a homosexual and declare the truth that God had created him to be a man. As he finished the Steps, he experienced
his freedom in Christ.

No, I didn't cast a demon of homosexuality out of him. I
don't believe there is a demon of homosexuality or a demon of
lust. That kind of simplistic thinking has hurt the credibility of
the church. I have seen Christianity mocked on prime-time
television by a parade of homosexuals and lesbians who have
left the church because well-meaning Christians have tried to
cast demons of homosexuality out of them.

Don't get me wrong—there is no question that Satan is a
player in our problems, and his hierarchy of demons will tempt,
accuse, deceive, and take advantage of any ground that is given
to them. But we must have a more wholistic answer if we are
going to see any lasting fruit.

We have identified God's design for sex and marriage. We
have seen how Satan attempts to pervert God's design and
direct our attention away from the Creator to self-centered
desires. We have considered the contributing factors to sexual
bondage and listed the steps that lead to a dark dead end. Hopefully, we are now ready to turn our attention to God's answer.

CHAPTER FIVE

The One-Step Program

The triumphant Christian does not fight for victory;
he celebrates a victory already won.

REGINALD WALLIS

I F GOD'S WORD SO CLEARLY COMMANDS people not to live in
sexual bondage, why don't we just obey God and stop doing
what He forbids? Because telling people that what they are
doing is wrong does not give them the power to stop doing it. Paul
declared, "If a law had been given that could impart life, then
righteousness would certainly have come by the law. But the
Scripture declares that the whole world is a prisoner of sin"
(Galatians 3:21-22).

Even more revealing is Paul's statement that "the sinful passions
aroused by the law were at work in our bodies" (Romans 7:5).
The law actually has the capacity to stimulate what it is intended
to prohibit. Forbidden fruit always appears more desirable. If you
don't believe it, tell your child he can go *here* but he can't go *there*.
The moment you say that, where does he want to go? *There!*
Laying down the law does not remove sinful passions. The core
problem is the basic nature of people—not their behavior, which
just reveals who they are and what they have chosen to believe.

The Pharisees were the most law-abiding people of Jesus' day, but they were far from righteous. Jesus told His disciples, "Unless your righteousness surpasses that of the Pharisees and the teachers of the law, you will certainly not enter the kingdom of heaven" (Matthew 5:20). Trying to live a righteous life externally when we are not righteous internally will only result in us becoming "whitewashed tombs, which look beautiful on the outside but on the inside are full of dead men's bones and everything unclean" (Matthew 23:27). The focus must be on what is inside, "for from within, out of men's hearts, come evil thoughts, sexual immorality, theft, murder, adultery, greed, malice, deceit, lewdness, envy, slander, arrogance, and folly. All these evils come from inside and make a man 'unclean'" (Mark 7:20-23).

The Secret of Victory: Our Identity in Christ

If trying harder to break the bonds of lustful thoughts and behavior and to live in sexual purity doesn't work, what will? Two verses in the Bible summarize what must happen in order for us to live righteously in Christ. First, "The reason the Son of God appeared was to destroy the devil's work. No one who is born of God will continue to sin, because God's seed remains in him" (1 John 3:8-9). If we are going to be set free from sexual bondage and walk in that freedom, our basic nature must be changed, and we must have a means for overcoming the evil one.

For those of us who are alive in Christ, these conditions have already been met, as the second verse tells us. God has made us partakers of His divine nature (2 Peter 1:4) and has provided the means by which we can live in victory over sin and Satan. What exactly happened to us?

Before we came to Christ, the following words described us:

> You were dead in your trespasses and sins, in which you formerly walked according to the course of this world, according to the prince of the power of

the air, of the spirit that is now working in the sons
of disobedience. Among them we too all formerly
lived in the lusts of our flesh, indulging the desires of
the flesh and of the mind, and were by nature children of wrath (Ephesians 2:1-3 NASB).

Before Christ, we were spiritually dead and under the domain of
Satan.

But a change took place at salvation. Paul wrote, "You were
once darkness, but now you are light in the Lord" (Ephesians
5:8). Our old nature in Adam was darkness; our new nature in
Christ is light. We have been transformed at the core of our
being. We are no longer "in the flesh"; we are "in Christ." Paul
wrote, "Those who are in the flesh cannot please God. However, you are not in the flesh but in the Spirit, if indeed the
Spirit of God dwells in you" (Romans 8:8-9 NASB).

Furthermore, before we became Christians we were under
the dominion of the god of this world, Satan. But the moment we
were saved, God "rescued us from the dominion of darkness and
brought us into the kingdom of the Son he loves, in whom we
have redemption, the forgiveness of sins" (Colossians 1:13-14).
We no longer have to serve Satan or sin. We "have been given
fullness in Christ, who is the head over every power and
authority" (Colossians 2:10). We are free to obey God and walk
in righteousness and purity.

All Our Needs Are Met in Christ

Paul says, "My God will meet all your needs according to his
glorious riches in Christ Jesus" (Philippians 4:19). The most
critical needs are the "being" needs, like eternal life. Jesus came
that we might have life (John 10:10)—spiritual or eternal life. To
be spiritually alive means that our souls are in union with God.
In the Bible, that truth is most often communicated by use of
the prepositional phrase "in Christ" or "in Him." And we have
a new identity: "To all who received him, to those who believed

in his name, he gave the right to become children of God"
(John 1:12). "How great is the love the Father has lavished on us,
that we should be called children of God! And that is what we
are!" (1 John 3:1).

Our foundational "being" needs of acceptance, security, and
significance are all met in Christ:

In Christ

I am accepted:

John 1:12	I am God's child
John 15:15	I am Jesus' chosen friend
Romans 5:1	I have been made holy and am accepted by God (justified)
1 Corinthians 6:17	I am united with the Lord and am one with Him in spirit
1 Corinthians 6:20	I have been bought with a price—I belong to God
1 Corinthians 12:27	I am a member of Christ's body— part of His family
Ephesians 1:1	I am a saint, a holy one
Ephesians 1:5	I have been adopted as God's child
Ephesians 2:18	I have direct access to God through the Holy Spirit
Colossians 1:14	I have been bought back (redeemed) and forgiven of all my sins
Colossians 2:10	I am complete in Christ

I am secure:

Romans 8:1-2	I am free from condemnation
Romans 8:28	I am assured that all things work together for good
Romans 8:31-34	I am free from any condemning charges against me

Romans 8:35-39	I cannot be separated from the love of God
2 Corinthians 1:21	I have been established, anointed, and sealed by God
Colossians 3:3	I am hidden with Christ in God
Philippians 1:6	I am assured that the good work that God has started in me will be finished
Philippians 3:20	I am a citizen of heaven
2 Timothy 1:7	I have not been given a spirit of fear, but of power, love, and a sound mind
Hebrews 4:16	I can find grace and mercy in time of need
1 John 5:18	I am born of God and the evil one cannot touch me

I am significant:

Matthew 5:13	I am the salt and light for everyone around me
John 15:1,5	I am a part of the true vine, joined to Christ and able to produce much fruit
John 15:16	I have been handpicked by Jesus to bear fruit
Acts 1:8	I am a personal witness of Christ's
1 Corinthians 3:16	I am God's temple, where the Holy Spirit lives
2 Corinthians 5:17-20	I am at peace with God, and He has given me the work of making peace between Himself and other people—I am a minister of reconciliation

2 Corinthians 6:1	I am God's co-worker
Ephesians 2:6	I am seated with Christ in the heavenlies
Ephesians 2:10	I am God's workmanship
Ephesians 3:12	I may approach God with freedom and confidence
Philippians 4:13	I can do all things through Christ who strengthens me

There is no way we can fix the failure and sin of the past, but by the grace of God we can be free from it. God's Word declares, "If anyone is in Christ, he is a new creation; the old has gone, the new has come!" (2 Corinthians 5:17). Furthermore, we are seated with Christ in the heavenlies, far above Satan's authority (Ephesians 2:4-6; Colossians 2:10-11), which means we have the authority to do God's will. But we also have a responsibility. We must *believe the truth* of who we are in Christ and *change how we live* as children of God.

The major problem with those living in bondage—sexual or other—is that they do not *see* the truths shared above. So Paul prays "that the eyes of your heart may be enlightened in order that you may know the hope to which he has called you, the riches of his glorious inheritance in the saints, and his incomparably great power for us who believe" (Ephesians 1:18-19). We already share in Christ's rich inheritance, and we already have the power to live victoriously in Christ. God has already accomplished for us what we could not do for ourselves.

My prayer also is that the eyes of your heart will be opened to see the inheritance and power God has provided for you in Christ. As we go on in this chapter you will discover more of what you must *believe* in order to experience your freedom from sexual bondage. In the next chapter you will learn how to *walk* in accordance with that liberating truth.

Paul's Teaching About Our Position in Christ

Paul argues in Romans 6:1-11 that what is true about Christ you should count as true about yourself also because you are alive "in Christ." (He further confirms this in 8:16-17: "The Spirit himself testifies with our spirit that we are God's children. Now if we are children, then we are heirs—heirs of God and co-heirs with Christ.") He also explains that if death has no mastery over us, then sin doesn't either.

When you read a command in the Bible, the only proper response is to obey it. When you find a promise in God's Word, you are to claim it. When Scripture is stating something that is true, the only proper response is for you to believe it. It's a simple concept, but many Christians try to do for themselves what Christ has already done for them. That should become clear as we discuss Paul's teaching here.

Further, the New Testament Greek language is precise concerning verb tenses. You can know when a verb is past, present, or future tense, and whether the verb is describing continuous action or an action that occurred at a point in time. However, you don't have to know the Greek language to appreciate what the Word of God is saying. Though the English translations bring this out fairly well, it is helpful to know that the verb tenses in Romans 6:1-10 are all past tense. In other words, this truth has already happened—and the only way we appropriately respond is by faith.

You Are Dead to Sin

Paul starts this passage by asking, "What shall we say, then? Shall we go on sinning so that grace may increase? By no means! We died to sin; how can we live in it any longer?" (verses 1-2). The defeated Christian asks, "How do I do that? How do I die to sin, including the sexual sins that have me bound?" The answer is, "You can't do it!" Why not? Because you have already died. You died to sin the moment you were born again. "We died to sin" is past tense. It has already happened for every child of God. This truth is something you must believe, not something you must do.

"I *can't* be dead to sin," you may respond, "because I don't *feel* dead to sin." You will have to set your feelings aside for a few verses, because it's what you believe that sets you free, not what you feel. God's Word is true whether you choose to believe it or not. Believing the Word of God doesn't make it true; His Word is true, therefore you must believe it even if your feelings don't match.

A pastor shared with me, "I have been struggling for 22 years in my Christian experience. It's been one trial after another, and I think I know what my problem is. I was doing my devotions the other day when I came across Colossians 3:3: 'You died, and your life is now hidden with Christ in God.' That's the key to victory, isn't it?" I assured him it was. Then he asked, "How do I do that?"

Surprised by his question, I asked him to look at the passage again and read it just a little more slowly. So he read it again: "'You died, and your life is hidden with Christ in God.'" Again he asked in desperation, "I know I need to die with Christ, but how do I do it?" This dear man had been desperately trying for 22 years to do something that has already been done—to become someone he already is. He's not alone. Many Bible-believing Christians are bogged down in their Christian walk because they have failed to understand their identity and position in Christ.

You Were Baptized into Christ's Death

Paul continues, "Don't you know that all of us who were baptized into Christ Jesus were baptized into his death?" (verse 3). Are you still wondering, *How do I do that?* The answer is the same: You can't do it, because you have already been baptized into Christ Jesus. It happened the moment you placed your faith in Jesus Christ as Savior and Lord. It is futile to seek something the Bible affirms we already have: "We were all baptized by one

Spirit into one body" (1 Corinthians 12:13). "We were" is past tense. It has already happened, Christian, so believe it.

This passage is addressing our spiritual baptism into Christ, of which the external ordinance practiced by most of our churches is a symbol—a symbolic representation of what has already been done. Augustine called baptism a "visible form of an invisible grace."

You Were Raised to New Life in Christ

"We were therefore buried with him through baptism into death in order that, just as Christ was raised from the dead through the glory of the Father, we too may live a new life. If we have been united with him like this in his death, we will certainly also be united with him in his resurrection" (verses 4-5). Have we been united with Him? Absolutely! "If we have been united with him" is, technically, a *first-class conditional clause*. It can literally be read, "If we have become united with Him in the likeness of His death—and we certainly have—we shall also be united with Him in the likeness of His resurrection."

Paul argues that we cannot receive only part of Jesus. You cannot identify with the death and burial of Christ without also identifying with His resurrection and ascension. You will live in defeat if you believe only half the gospel. You have died with Christ, *and* you have been raised with Him and seated with Him in the heavenlies (Ephesians 2:6). From this position you have all the authority and power you need to live the Christian life. Every child of God is spiritually alive "in Christ" and is identified with Him

- in His death (Romans 6:3,6; Galatians 2:20; Colossians 3:1-3)
- in His burial (Romans 6:4)
- in His resurrection (Romans 6:5,8,11)
- in His ascension (Ephesians 2:6)

- in His life (Romans 5:10-11)
- in His power (Ephesians 1:19-20)
- in His inheritance (Romans 8:16-17; Ephesians 1:11-12)

Jesus didn't come only to die for our sins; He also came to give us life (John 10:10). If all we understand is the crucifixion, then we will perceive ourselves as "forgiven sinners" instead of redeemed saints—that is, *children of God*. We celebrate the resurrection of Jesus Christ on Easter, not just His death on Good Friday. It is the resurrected life of Christ that we are to abide in.

Notice how Paul unfolds this truth in Romans 5:8-11. "God demonstrates his own love for us in this: While we were still sinners, Christ died for us" (verse 8). Isn't that great, Christian? God loves you! But is that all? No! "Since we have now been justified by his blood, *how much more* shall we be saved from God's wrath through him!" (verse 9).

Isn't that great, Christian? You're not going to hell! But is that all? No! "For if, when we were God's enemies, we were reconciled to him through the death of his Son, *how much more*, having been reconciled, shall we be saved through his life!" (verse 10).

Isn't that great, Christian? You have been saved by His life. Eternal life isn't something you get when you die. You are alive in Christ right now. But is that all? No! "Not only is this so, but we also rejoice in God through our Lord Jesus Christ, through whom we have now received reconciliation" (verse 11). This reconciliation assures us that our souls are in union with God, which is what it means to be spiritually alive.

Peter also affirms this incredible truth:

> His divine power has given us everything we need for life and godliness through our knowledge of him who called us by his own glory and goodness. Through these he has given us his very great and precious promises, so that through them you may participate in the divine nature and escape the

corruption in the world caused by evil desires"
(2 Peter 1:3-4).

Are you beginning to see a glimmer of hope for overcoming
sexual bondage? You should be, because you have already died to
it and have been raised to new and victorious life in Christ.

Your Old Self Was Crucified with Christ

Paul continues, "For we know that our old self was crucified
with him so that the body of sin might be done away with, that
we should no longer be slaves to sin" (6:6). The text does not say
"we must do." It says, "we *know*." Your old self was crucified with
Christ. The only proper response to this powerful truth is to
believe it. Many people are desperately trying to put to death
the old self—with all its tendencies to sin—but they can't do it.
Why not? Because it is already dead! You cannot do for yourself
what God alone can and has already done for you.

Christians who continually fail in their Christian experience
begin to reason incorrectly and ask "What experience must I
undergo in order for me to live victoriously?" There is none.
The only experience that was necessary for this verse to be true
occurred over 2000 years ago on the cross. And the only way we
can enter into that experience today is by faith. We can't save
ourselves, and we can't overcome the penalty of death or the
power of sin by human effort. Only God can do that for us, and
He has already done it.

As I was explaining this truth during a conference, a man
raised his hand and said, "I've been a Christian for 13 years.
Why hasn't someone told me this before?" Maybe no one had
shared with him, or maybe he hadn't been listening. Don't
think that this is just "positional truth," which implies that
there is little or no present-day benefit in being alive and free in
Christ. This is not pie-in-the-sky theology. This is the only basis
for our hope of ever living a righteous life. If we choose to
believe it and live accordingly by faith, the truth of this passage

will work itself out in our experience. Trying to make it true by our experience will lead to defeat.

We don't live obediently hoping that God may someday accept us. We are already accepted by God, so we live obediently. We don't labor in God's vineyard hoping that He may someday love us. God already loves us, so we joyfully labor in His vineyard. It is not what we do that determines who we are— it is who we are and what we believe that determines what we do.

You Have Been Freed from Sin

"Anyone who has died has been freed from sin" (6:7). Have you died with Christ? Then you are free from sin. You may be thinking, *I don't feel free from sin.* If you only believe what you feel, you will never live a victorious life. In all honesty, I wake up some mornings feeling very alive to sin and very dead to Christ. But that's just the way I feel. If I believed what I feel and walked that way the rest of my day, what kind of a day do you think I would have? It would be a pretty bad day!

I have learned to greet each new day by praying, *Dear Lord, I deserved eternal damnation, but You gave me eternal life. I ask You to fill me with Your Holy Spirit, and I choose to walk by faith regardless of how I feel. I know I will face many temptations today, but I choose to take every thought captive to the obedience of Christ and to think upon that which is true and right.*

A seminary student asked me, "Are you telling me I don't have to sin?"

I responded, "Where did you get the idea you have to sin?" I read 1 John 2:1 to him: "My dear children, I write this to you so that you will not sin. But if anybody does sin, we have one who speaks to the Father in our defense—Jesus Christ, the Righteous One." God does not refer to us in Scripture as sinners. We are clearly identified as saints who still have the capacity to sin.

Obviously, Christian maturity is a factor in our ability to stand against temptation, but what an incredible sense of defeat must accompany the belief that we are bound to sin when God commands us not to sin! Many people in sexual bondage are caught in this hopeless web. They think, *God, You made me this way—and now You condemn me for it. Unfair!* That would be unfair, but God didn't create Adam and Eve to be alive physically and dead spiritually. They chose to separate themselves from God by their own sin. We also have made choices to sin, and we will never recover unless we assume responsibility for our actions and attitudes.

God has done all He needs to do for us to live victorious lives in Christ. It is equally wrong to say, "The Christian life is impossible!" Then when those who say this fail, they proclaim, "I'm only human!" They believe the lie that the scope of the gospel isn't big enough to include sexual bondage. Such thinking reflects a faulty belief system. We have been saved, not by how we *behave*, but by how we *believe*. This is a paradox and stumbling block to the natural mind. But to biblically informed Christians, it is the basis for our freedom and conquest—our union with God and our walk by faith.

There is no greater sin than the sin of unbelief. On more than one occasion the Lord made statements like "according to your faith will it be done to you" (Matthew 9:29). Paul wrote, "Everything that does not come from faith is sin" (Romans 14:23). If we choose to believe a lie, we will live a lie, but if we choose to believe the truth, we will live a victorious life by faith—that is, by the same means by which we were saved.

Death Is No Longer Your Master

"If we died with Christ, we believe that we will also live with him. For we know that since Christ was raised from the dead, he cannot die again; death no longer has mastery over him" (6:8-9). Does death have mastery over any believer? Absolutely not! Why? Because death could not master Christ, and you are alive in Him. " 'Death has been swallowed up in victory.' 'Where, O death, is your victory? Where, O death, is your sting?' The sting of death is sin, and power of sin is the law. But thanks be to God! He gives us the victory through our Lord Jesus Christ" (1 Corinthians 15:54-57).

Since Christ has triumphed over death by His resurrection, death has no mastery over us who are spiritually alive in Christ Jesus. Jesus said, "I am the resurrection and the life. He who believes in me will live [spiritually], even though he dies [physically]; and whoever lives and believes in me will never die [spiritually]. Do you believe this?" (John 11:25-26). Do you believe what Jesus said? Then be it done to you according to how you believe!

A Once-for-All Death

Paul continues, "The death he died, he died to sin once for all; but the life he lives, he lives to God" (6:10). This was accomplished when "God made him who had no sin to be sin for us, so that in him we might become the righteousness of God" (2 Corinthians 5:21). When Jesus went to the cross, when they nailed those spikes into His hands and feet, the Father was in the process of laying all the sins of the world upon Him. But when He was resurrected, there were no sins upon Him. They stayed in the grave. As He sits at the right hand of the Father today, there are no sins upon Him. Jesus has triumphed over sin and death. Since you are alive in Him, you are also dead to sin.

Many Christians accept the truth that Christ died for the sins they have already committed, but what about the sins they commit in the future? When Christ died for all your sins, how many of your sins were then future? All of them! This is not a license to sin, which is the basis for our addictions, but a marvelous truth on which to stand against Satan's accusations. It is the truth we must know in order to live free in Christ.

The One-Step Response

In 6:11, Paul summarizes how we are to respond to what Christ has accomplished for us by His death and resurrection:

"In the same way, count yourselves dead to sin but alive to God in Christ Jesus." We do not make ourselves dead to sin by considering it to be so. We consider ourselves dead to sin because God says it already is so. The King James Version of the same verse reads, "Reckon yourselves to be dead unto sin." If you think that your reckoning makes you dead to sin, you will reckon yourself into a wreck! We can't make ourselves dead to sin; only God can do that—and He has already done it. Paul is saying we must keep on choosing to believe by faith what God says is true, even when our feelings say otherwise.

The verb "count" (or "reckon") is present tense. In other words, we must continuously believe this truth and daily affirm we are dead to sin and alive in Christ. This is essentially the same thing as abiding in Christ (John 15:1-8) and walking by the Spirit (Galatians 5:16). As we take our stand in the truth of what God has done and who we are in Christ, we will not easily be deceived or be led to carry out the desires of the flesh.

Living Under a Greater Law

Has sin disappeared because we have died to it? No. Has the power of sin diminished? No, it is still strong and still appealing. But when sin makes its appeal, we have the power to say no to it because our relationship with sin ended when the Lord "rescued us from the dominion of darkness and brought us into the kingdom of the Son he loves" (Colossians 1:13). Paul explains how this is possible in Romans 8:1-2: "There is now no condemnation for those who are in Christ Jesus, because through Christ Jesus the law of the Spirit of life set me free from the law of sin and death."

Is the law of sin and death still operative? Yes, and that is why Paul calls it a law. But it has been overcome by a greater law—"the law of the Spirit of life in Christ Jesus." It's like flying. Can you fly by your own power? No, because the law of gravity keeps you bound to earth. But you *can* fly in an airplane, which has a power greater than the law of gravity. As long as you remain in the airplane you can fly. If you jump out at 20,000 feet and try flying on your own, you will crash and burn.

Like gravity, the law of sin and death is still here, still operative, still powerful, and still making its appeal. But you don't need to submit to it. The law of the Spirit of life is a greater law. As long as you live by the Spirit, you will not carry out the desires of the flesh (Galatians 5:16). You must "be strong in the Lord and in his mighty power" (Ephesians 6:10). The moment you think you can stand on your own, the moment you stop depending on the Lord, you are headed for a fall (Proverbs 16:18).

All temptation is an attempt by the devil to get us to live our lives independently of God. "So, if you think you are standing firm, be careful that you don't fall! No temptation has seized you except what is common to man. And God is faithful; he will not let you be tempted beyond what you can bear. But when you are tempted, he will also provide a way out so that you can stand up under it" (1 Corinthians 10:12-13). When we succumb to temptation and are deceived by the father of lies, we should quickly repent of our sin, renounce the lies, return to our loving Father—who cleanses us—and resume the walk of faith.

Perhaps you have struggled in defeat against sexual sin and bondage while vainly trying to figure out what you must do to get free. I hope the truth of Romans 6:1-11 has blown away the prison doors in your understanding. It's not what you do that sets you free—it's what Christ has already done and what you are now choosing to believe. God has done everything that needs to be done through the death and resurrection of Jesus Christ. Your vital first step to freedom is to believe that, claim it, and stake your life on it.

CHAPTER SIX

Overcoming Sin's Entrapment

*It is absolutely certain that if a man sins, his own sin
will dog him, that it will keep on his track night and
day, like a bloodhound, and never quit until it catches
him and brings him to account.*

R.A. TORREY

As with many victims, Melissa's memories of sexual abuse
were blocked by the trauma she had experienced. However, her
negative view of herself and abnormal childhood behavior sig-
naled a deep, hidden problem, as we see from her story:

> I felt so inadequate and unacceptable as a child. I
> avoided getting close to anyone, especially boys, fearing
> they would find out how terrible I was. Everyone seemed
> to react to me in a sexual way. When I was a girl of six or
> seven, men whispered to me what they wanted to do to
> me when I got older. As I grew up, women seemed
> threatened by me, as if I intended to steal their husbands.
> This behavior only reinforced my belief there was some-
> thing wrong with me and everyone saw it. I had become
> a Christian as a young child, but I was convinced God
> had picked me out to be sexually tormented and
> abused.

About the time I turned nine or ten, I began to experiment with masturbation. I also became quite self-destructive. I cut the insides of my legs and put alcohol on the wounds to make them hurt more. I cut pieces of skin off my knuckles just to feel the pain I knew I deserved. As a young teen I was shy and afraid of boys. I didn't have many friends. When I dated, I either froze up after a little bit of necking or blanked out, unable to remember what I did or how I got home. I became bulimic at about 14.

I rededicated my life to Christ at age 15. But as I left high school and entered college I continued to binge and purge once or twice a day. I also strayed into a few sexual involvements, and most of those guys were also Christians. I wanted to be loved and accepted, so I gave them my body. But when I did, the boys just used me and discarded me. With or without sex, the boys rejected me. I felt dirty and trapped.

When Melissa married Dan in her early twenties, their physical intimacy opened a floodgate of memories and nightmares about her clouded past. She dreamed about her grandfather raping her while her new husband watched with enjoyment. Gradually the repressed memories of her horrifying past came into focus.

She recalled being molested by her grandfather at age two. She was forced to accept and perform oral sex and other atrocities with him as a young child. At the time she was cutting herself, she was also awakened often in the middle of the night by severe abdominal pain. An insightful doctor told Melissa's mother that she was being sexually abused. The mother blamed Melissa's stepfather, brother, and uncle—everyone but her grandfather, the man who was doing it.

Melissa felt betrayed by the doctor for revealing her "secret." She had never considered telling anyone how Grandpa "loved" her, even though she felt it was wrong. She was confused. She loved her grandfather, but she also prayed that God would kill him to make the abuse stop. When he did die before Melissa became a teenager, she felt responsible and mourned him. But the inner wounds he had inflicted continued to torment her for years.

The Way Out of the Trap

Sexual abuse devastates us as a whole person. It distorts our worldview and our concept of God and ourselves. Studies show that nearly half of all female children will experience some form of sexual abuse before they reach their fourteenth birthday.[5] Furthermore, the perpetrators of 85 to 94 percent of sexual violations are either relatives, family friends, neighbors, or acquaintances of the victim, not strangers.[6] The abused come to Christ, hear the truth...but they can't seem to appropriate it. Both the abused and the abuser are trapped in the "sin-confess-sin-confess-and-sin-again" cycle. In most cases they have failed to deal with sin's entrapment.

In the previous chapter we looked at Romans 6:1-11 and learned what Christ has already done for us—but we have a responsibility as well, and Paul shares that in Romans 6:12-13. But take caution—what God calls you to do in verses 12 and 13 will not be effective if you're not believing what Paul teaches in verses 1 through 11. *Truth sets us free* from sexual and all bondages, and *believing the truth* precedes responsible behavior.

Give Yourself as an Offering

Based on his previous teaching in Romans 6, Paul gives a specific assignment to all believers: "Therefore do not let sin reign in your mortal body so that you obey its evil desires" (verse 12). According to this verse, it is our responsibility to not allow sin to reign in our mortal bodies. We cannot say, "The devil made me do it," or that anyone else did for that matter. God never commands us to do something we cannot do, and the devil can't prevent us from doing it. In Christ, you have died to sin—and the devil can't *make* you do anything. He will tempt you, accuse you, and try to deceive you—but if sin reigns in your body, it does so because *you* allowed it to happen. You are responsible for your own attitudes and actions.

How then do we prevent sin from reigning in our bodies? Paul answers in verse 13: "Do not offer the parts of your body to sin, as instruments of wickedness, but rather offer yourselves to God, as those who have been brought from death to life; and offer the parts of your body to him as instruments of righteousness." Notice that there is only one negative action to avoid, and two positive actions to practice.

Don't offer the parts of your body to sin. We are not to use our eyes, hands, feet, or any part of our bodies in any way that would serve sin. When you see a sexually explicit program on TV and lustfully watch it, you are offering your body to sin. When you get inappropriately "touchy-feely" with a co-worker of the opposite sex, you are offering your body to sin. When you fantasize sexually about someone other than your spouse, you are offering your body to sin. Whenever you choose to offer parts of your body to sin, you invite sin to rule in your physical body. "What is the source of quarrels and conflicts among you? Is not the source your pleasures that wage war in your members?" (James 4:1 NASB).

Offer yourself and the parts of your body to God. Notice that Paul makes a distinction between "yourselves" and "the parts of your body." What is the distinction? Self is who we are on the inside—the immaterial or inner person that is being renewed day by day (2 Corinthians 4:16). Our bodies and their various parts are who we are on the outside, the mortal, temporal part of us. Someday we are going to jettison our old "earth suits." At that time we will be absent from our mortal bodies and present with the Lord in immortal bodies (2 Corinthians 5:8). As long as we are on planet Earth, however, our inner selves are united with our outer physical bodies. We are to offer the complete package—body, soul, and spirit—to God.

Paul wrote, "The body that is sown is perishable, it is raised imperishable; it is sown in dishonor, it is raised in glory; it is sown in weakness, it is raised in power; it is sown a natural body, it is raised a spiritual body" (1 Corinthians 15:42-44). Our inner man will live forever with our heavenly Father, but our bodies won't. Paul continues: "Flesh and blood cannot inherit the kingdom of God, nor does the perishable inherit the imperishable" (verse 50). That which is mortal is corruptible.

Is our physical body evil? No, it's amoral, or neutral. So what are we to do about the neutral disposition of our bodies? We are instructed to present them to God "as instruments of righteousness." To "present" means to place at the disposal of. An instrument can be anything the Lord has entrusted to us, including our bodies. For example, your car is an amoral, neutral instrument for your use. You can use your car for good or bad purposes—you can choose to drive people to church or to sell drugs. Similarly, your body can be used for good or evil purposes as you choose. You have opportunities every day to offer your eyes, your hands, your brain, your feet, and so on, to sin or to God. The Lord commands us to be good stewards of our bodies and use them only as instruments of righteousness. Ultimately, it's our choice.

Your Body, God's Temple

In 1 Corinthians 6:13-20, Paul offers a little more body theology, especially as it relates to sexual immorality:

> The body is not meant for sexual immorality, but for the Lord, and the Lord for the body. By his power God raised the Lord from the dead, and he will raise us also. Do you not know that your bodies are members of Christ himself? Shall I then take the members of Christ and unite them with a prostitute?

> Never! Do you not know that he who unites himself with a prostitute is one with her in body? For it is said, "The two will become one flesh." But he who unites himself with the Lord is one with him in spirit.
>
> Flee from sexual immorality. All other sins a man commits are outside his body, but he who sins sexually sins against his own body. Do you not know that your body is a temple of the Holy Spirit, who is in you, whom you have received from God? You are not your own; you were bought at a price. Therefore honor God with your body.

This passage teaches that we have more than a spiritual union with God. Our bodies are members of Christ Himself. Romans 8:11 declares, "If the Spirit of him who raised Jesus from the dead is living in you, he who raised Christ from the dead will also give life to your mortal bodies through his Spirit, who lives in you." Our bodies are actually God's temple because His Spirit dwells in us. To use our bodies for sexual immorality is to defile the temple of God.

It is hard for us to fully understand the moral outrage felt in heaven when one of God's children uses His temple as an instrument of unrighteousness. It is even worse when someone defiles the temple of another person through rape or incest. It compares to the despicable act of Antiochus Epiphanes in the second century before Christ. This godless Syrian ruler overran Jerusalem, declared the Mosaic ceremonies illegal, erected a statue of Zeus in the Temple, and slaughtered a pig—an unclean animal—on the altar. Can you imagine how God's people must have felt to have their holy place so thoroughly desecrated? Have you ever felt the same way about defiling God's temple, which is our bodies?

As a Christian, aren't you offended when people suggest that Jesus was sexually intimate with Mary Magdalene? Jesus was fully God, but He was also fully man. He was tempted in every way we are, including sexually, but He never sinned. His earthly body was not meant for sexual immorality, and neither is ours. If our eyes were fully open to the reality of the spiritual world and we understood the violation felt in heaven when we sin against our own bodies, we would more quickly obey the Scripture's command to flee from sexual immorality.

Can you think of any way you could commit a sexual sin and not use your body as an instrument of unrighteousness? I can't. Therefore, when we do commit a sexual sin, we allow sin to reign in our mortal bodies! Are we still united with the Lord? Yes, because He will never leave us nor forsake us. We don't lose our salvation, but we certainly lose our daily victory. Paul urges us, "You were called to freedom, brethren; only do not turn your freedom into an opportunity for the flesh, but through love serve one another" (Galatians 5:13 NASB).

An Immoral Bond

What happens when a child of God—who is united with the Lord and one spirit with Him—also "unites himself with a prostitute" through sexual immorality? The Bible says they become one flesh. Somehow they bond together. Bonding is a positive thing in a wholesome relationship, but in an immoral union, bonding only leads to bondage.

How many times have you heard of an upright Christian young woman who becomes involved with an immoral man, has sex with him, and then continues in a sick relationship with him for two or three or more years? He may mistreat her, and friends and relatives tell her, "He's no good for you. Get rid of the bum!" But she won't listen to them. Even though he treats her badly, the woman won't leave him. Why? Because a spiritual and emotional bond has been formed. The two of them have become one flesh. Such bonds must be broken in Christ.

This spiritual and emotional bond can occur as a result of heavy petting or oral sex. At a conference, a colleague and I counseled a young husband and wife who were experiencing marital problems. Even though they were committed to each other, their sexual relationship had been dull and lifeless since their wedding. Both husband and wife had been romantically involved before marriage with other partners, though without intercourse.

During our counseling session, both husband and wife admitted for the first time that they were still emotionally attached to their "first loves." At our encouragement, they renounced petting and romantic involvement with their previous partners and recommitted their lives and their bodies to the Lord. They further committed to reserve the sexual use of their bodies for each other only. The next day they shared with me that they had had a joyful, intimate encounter with each other that night—a first for their marriage. Once the sexual and emotional bonds had been broken, they were free to enjoy each other the way God intended.

In the Steps to Freedom in Christ, we encourage the people we counsel to pray and ask the Lord to reveal every sexual use of their bodies as instruments of unrighteousness—and God does. Then for each one God brings to mind, they pray, "I renounce that use of my body with (the person's name), and I ask you to break that sexual bond." If there has been an emotional attachment, they pray, "...break that sexual and emotional bond." Then they are urged to give their bodies to God as living sacrifices and pray that God would fill them with His Holy Spirit. Finally, they are encouraged to forgive those who have offended them. They forgive others for their own sakes, since nothing will keep you more bound to the past than unforgiveness. To forgive is to set a captive free and then realize you were the captive.

I mentioned earlier that in the cases of rape and incest, a person's temple is also defiled, even though they are innocent. "Not fair!" you say. Of course it isn't fair—it is a violation of that person's temple. They have been victimized, but they don't have to remain a victim. They can renounce that use of their body and give it to God as a living sacrifice. Complete freedom comes when they have forgiven their abuser and have let God be the avenger.

I was asked by a local pastor to counsel a young lady who was hearing voices in her head. They were so audible to her that she couldn't understand why we couldn't hear them. She had lived with a man who had abused her. He dealt drugs for a living. She was now living at home but was still attached to him. I first asked her what she would do if we asked her to make a commitment to never see him again. She said, "I would probably get up and leave." I suspected that would be the case, but I wanted the pastor to hear it. Having her make such a commitment was a legitimate goal, but at that point the timing was wrong.

After hearing her story, I asked if she would like to resolve her conflicts and find her freedom in Christ. She wholeheartedly agreed, and I took her through the Steps. When we were done, there were no more demonic voices in her head, and she seemed to be in complete peace. Finally she remarked, "I am never going to see that man again." That conviction had come from God, but it hadn't come until she had fully repented. Trying to get other people, such as our children, to make behavioral changes without inner conviction won't work.

Offering Yourself to God

Wonderful things happen when we determine to offer our body to God as an instrument of righteousness instead of offering our body to sin. The Bible's sacrificial system provides a beautiful illustration.

The sin offering in the Old Testament was a blood offering. Blood was drained from the sacrificial animal, and the carcass was taken outside the camp and disposed of. Only the blood was offered to God for the forgiveness of sin. Hebrews 9:22 states, "Without the shedding of blood there is no forgiveness."

At the cross, the Lord Jesus Christ became our sin offering. After He shed His blood for us, His body was taken down and buried outside the city, but unlike the slain lamb of the Old Testament, the Lamb of God did not stay buried for long.

The other primary offering in the Old Testament was a burnt offering. Unlike the sin offering, the burnt offering was totally consumed on the altar—blood, carcass, everything. In the Hebrew language, *burnt* literally means "that which ascends." In the burnt offering, the whole sacrificial animal ascended to God in flames and smoke from the altar. It was "an aroma pleasing to the LORD" (Leviticus 1:9).

Jesus is the sin offering, but who is the burnt offering? We are! Paul writes, "I urge you, brothers, in view of God's mercy, to offer your bodies as living sacrifices, holy and pleasing to God—this is your spiritual act of worship" (Romans 12:1). It's wonderful to know that our sins are forgiven; Christ did that for us when He shed His blood. But if you want to live victoriously in Christ over the sin that plagues you, you must present yourself to God and present your body as an instrument of righteousness. Such a sacrifice is "pleasing to God," as the aroma of the burnt offering was in the Old Testament.

To illustrate this, consider the spiritual revival under King Hezekiah, as recorded in 2 Chronicles 29. First, Hezekiah cleaned out the temple and prepared it for worship by purifying it. This is a picture of repentance. Under the New Covenant believers are the temple of God. Second, the king consecrated the priests. In the New Testament, every child of God is part of the priesthood of believers. This also parallels Paul's instruction to present ourselves to God. Third, Hezekiah ordered the blood offering for the forgiveness of sins. Nothing visible happened during the blood offering, but according to God's law, the sins of the people were forgiven. Then "Hezekiah gave the order to sacrifice the burnt offering on the altar. As the offering began, singing to the LORD began also...All this continued until the sacrifice of the burnt offering was completed" (verses 27-28). The burnt offering was such a significant and worshipful event that it was surrounded by music in the temple. The account concludes, "Hezekiah and all the people rejoiced at what God had brought about for his people" (verse 36). Great joy results when believers obediently and wholeheartedly present themselves and their bodies to God.

It is not enough to have our sins forgiven—we must be filled with God's Holy Spirit. Notice what happens when we are filled, according to Ephesians 5:18-20:

> Do not get drunk on wine, which leads to debauchery. Instead, be filled with the Spirit. Speak to one another with psalms, hymns and spiritual songs. Sing and make music in your heart to the Lord, always giving thanks to God the Father for everything.

Just as in the Old Testament, music fills the temple when we yield ourselves to God.

Winning the Struggle with Sin

The music sounding inside sexually bound Christians is more like a funeral dirge than a song of joy. They feel defeated instead of victorious. They have offered their bodies as instruments of sexual sin and feel hopelessly trapped in sexual bondage. They may experience occasional periods of relief and success at saying no to temptation—but sin is reigning in their mortal bodies, and they can't seem to get out of the sin-confess-and-sin-again cycle. Perhaps you find yourself in this discouraging condition.

Paul describes this struggle in Romans 7:15-25. The conversation that follows is based on many counseling sessions I have had with Christians struggling with temptation, sin, and bondage. You may find yourself identifying with Dan as I talk him through Paul's teaching.* I trust you will also identify with the liberating truth of God's Word.[7]

---

*All Scripture quotations in the conversation are from the NASB.

Dan: Neil, I can't keep going on like this. I have been sexually promiscuous in the past, and I'm really sorry about it. I have confessed it to the Lord, but I can't seem to get victory over it. I commit myself to avoid pornography. But the temptation is overwhelming and I give in to it. I don't want to live like this! It's ruining my marriage.

Neil: Dan, let's look at a passage of Scripture that seems to describe what you are experiencing. Romans 7:15 reads, "What I am doing, I do not understand; for I am not practicing what I would like to do, but I am doing the very thing I hate." Would you say that pretty well describes your life?

Dan: Exactly! I really want to do what God says is right, and I hate being in bondage to this lust. I sneak down at night and call one of those sex hotlines, or I turn on my computer and get on the Internet. Afterward I feel disgusted with myself.

Neil: It sounds like you would identify with verse 16 as well: "But if I do the very thing I do not want to do, I agree with the Law, confessing that the Law is good." Dan, how many persons are mentioned in this verse?

Dan: There is only one person, and it is clearly "I."

Neil: It can be very defeating to know what we want to do, but for some reason not be able to do it. How have you tried to resolve this conflict?

Dan: Sometimes I wonder if I'm even a Christian. It seems to work for others but not for me. I sometimes doubt if the Christian life is possible or if God is really here.

Neil: You're not alone, Dan. Many Christians believe they are different from others, and most think they are the only ones who struggle with sexual temptations. If you were the only player in this battle, it would stand to reason that you would question your salvation or the existence of God. But look at verse 17: "So now, no longer am I the one doing it, but sin which dwells in me." Now how many players are there?

Dan: Apparently two, "I" and "sin." But I don't understand. Aren't *I* and *sin* the same?

Neil: Sometimes we *feel* like sin, but *we* are not sin. The Bible teaches that if we say we have no sin, we deceive ourselves (1 John 1:8). But *having* sin and *being* sin are two totally different issues. Now let's read verse 18 and see if we can make some sense out of it: "I know that nothing good dwells in me, that is, in my flesh; for the willing is present in me, but the doing of the good is not."

Dan: I learned that verse a long time ago. It's been easy for me to figure out that I'm no good for myself and no good for my wife. Sometimes I think it would be better if I just weren't here.

Neil: That's not true, because that's not what the verse says. In fact, it says the opposite. The "nothing good" that is dwelling in you is not *you.* It's something else. If I had a wood splinter in my finger, it would be "nothing good" dwelling in me. But the "nothing good" isn't me; it's a splinter. It's important to note that the "nothing good" is not even my flesh—rather, it is operating *in* my flesh ("sin nature"). If we see only ourselves in this struggle, living righteously will seem hopeless. This passage is going to great lengths to tell us there is a second party involved in our struggle, whose nature is evil and different from ours.

You see, Dan, when you and I were born, we were born under the penalty of sin. And we know that Satan and his emissaries are always working to keep us under that penalty. When God saved us, Satan lost that battle, but he didn't curl up his tail or pull in his fangs. He is now committed to keeping us under the power of sin. But in Christ we have died to sin and are no longer under its power.

In 1 John 2:12-14, the apostle John writes to little children because their sins are forgiven. In other words, they have overcome the penalty of sin. He writes to young men because they have overcome the evil one. In other words, they have overcome the power of sin. We have the authority in Christ to experience our victory over the penalty and power of sin, despite Satan's lies to the contrary. Romans 7 also says that this evil is going to work through the flesh, which remains with us after our salvation. It is our responsibility to crucify the flesh and to resist the devil.

Let's continue in the passage to see if we can learn more about how the battle is being waged. Verses 19-21 state, "For the good that I want, I do not do; but I practice the very evil that I do not want. But if I am doing the very thing I do not want, I am no longer the one doing it, but sin which dwells in me. I find then the principle that evil is present in me, the one who wants to do good."

Dan, can you identify from these verses the nature of the "nothing good" that dwells in you?

Dan: Sure, it is clearly evil and sin. But isn't it just my own sin? When I sin, I feel guilty.

Neil: There's no question that you and I sin, but we are not "sin" as such. Evil is present in us, but Paul is not calling us evil. In fact, he is making a clear distinction between *us* and the sin that is dwelling *in* us. This does not excuse us from sinning, because Paul wrote in Romans 6:12 that we are responsible not to let sin reign in our mortal bodies.

Dan, let me share another example of this passage. Consider women who struggle with eating disorders. Many of them cut themselves, force themselves to defecate, and binge and purge. They do this because they are deceived into believing there is evil present in them, and they are trying to get it out. But cutting themselves or defecating or purging won't get rid of this kind of evil. The lies they have believed are exposed when they renounce defecating or purging or cutting themselves as a means of cleansing themselves—and trust only in the cleansing work of Christ. When you came under conviction about your sexual sin, what did you do?

Dan: I confessed it to God.

Neil: Dan, confession literally means "to agree with God." It is the same thing as walking in the light, or living in moral agreement with Him about our present condition. We must confess our sin if we are going to live in harmony with our heavenly

Father, but that doesn't go far enough. Confession is only the first step to repentance. The man that Paul is writing about agrees with God that what he is doing is wrong, but that doesn't resolve his problem. You have confessed your sin to God, but you are still in bondage to lust. It has to be very frustrating for you. Have you ever felt so defeated that you just lash out at someone or at yourself?

Dan: Almost every day!

Neil: But when you cool down, do you again entertain thoughts that are in line with who you really are as a child of God?

Dan: Always, and then I feel terrible about lashing out.

Neil: Verse 22 explains why: "For I joyfully concur with the law of God in the inner man." When we act out of character with who we really are, the Holy Spirit immediately brings conviction because of our union with God. Out of frustration and failure, we think or say things like "I'm not going back to church anymore." "Christianity doesn't work." "It was God who made me this way, and now I feel condemned all the time." "God promised to provide a way of escape. Well, where is it? I haven't found it!" But soon our true nature begins to express itself: "I know what I'm doing is wrong, and I know God loves me—but I'm so frustrated by my continuing failure."

Dan: Someone told me once that this passage was talking about a non-Christian.

Neil: I know some people who take that position, but it doesn't make sense to me. Does a natural man joyfully concur with the law of God in the inner man? Does an unbeliever agree with the law of God and confess that it is good? I don't think so! In fact, they speak out rather strongly against it. Some even hate us Christians for upholding such a moral standard.

Now look at verse 23, which describes the nature of this battle with sin: "But I see a different law in the members of my body, waging war against the law of my mind and making me a prisoner of the law of sin which is in my members." According to this passage, Dan, where is the battle being fought?

Dan: The battle appears to be in the mind.

Neil: That's precisely where the battle rages. Now if Satan can get you to think you are the only one in the battle, you will get down on yourself or God when you sin, which is counterproductive to resolving the problem. Let me put it this way: Suppose you opened a door you were told not to open, and a dog came through the door and wrapped his teeth around your leg. Would you beat on yourself, or would you beat on the dog?

Dan: I suppose I would beat on the dog.

Neil: Of course you would. On the other side of the door, another dog—Satan—is tempting you with thoughts like "Come on, open the door. I have an exciting video to show you." "Everybody else is doing it. You'll get away with it." So you open the door, and the dog comes in and grabs hold of your leg. You feel the pain of conviction as soon as you open the door, and the tempter switches to being the accuser. Your mind is pummeled by his accusations: "You opened the door. You're a miserable excuse for a Christian. God certainly can't love someone as sinful as you."

So you cry out, "God, forgive me!" He does—actually, you are *already* forgiven. But the dog is still clinging to your leg! You are stuck in the cycle of sin-confess-sin-confess-sin-confess. You beat on yourself continually for your repeated failure.

People eventually get tired of beating on themselves, so they walk away from God under a cloud of defeat and condemnation. Paul expressed this feeling in verse 24: "Wretched man that I am! Who will set me free from the body of this death?" He doesn't say he's wicked or sinful, but that he's miserable. This man is not experiencing his freedom. His attempts to do the right thing are met with moral failure because he has submitted to God but has not resisted the devil (James 4:7). There is nobody more miserable than someone who knows what is right and wants to do what is right—but can't seem to do it.

Dan: That's me—miserable!

Neil: Wait a minute, Dan. There is victory. Jesus will set us free. Look at verse 25: "Thanks be to God through Jesus Christ our Lord! So then, on the one hand I myself with my mind am serving the law of God, but on the other, with my flesh the law of sin." Let's go back to the dog illustration. Why isn't crying out to God enough to solve your ongoing conflict with sexual sin?

Dan: Well, like you said, the dog is still there. I guess I have to chase off the dog.

Neil: You will also have to close the door. That means you get rid of all your pornography and cut off any future supply, including the Internet. If you have a sexual partner other than your wife, you must call her right now and tell her it's over.

Dan: But…I owe her an explanation. I'll just meet with her once, and that will be that.

Neil: That won't work, Dan. You have to call her right now in my presence and commit yourself to never see or contact her again. You owe an explanation to your wife—no one else.

Dan: Okay, give me the phone…

———

Neil: Now that you've dealt with that relationship, here are the steps you must take:

First, realize that you are already forgiven. Christ died once for all your sins. You were right in confessing your sin to God because you need to own up to the fact that you opened the door when you knew it was wrong.

Second, to make sure that every door is closed, you need to ask the Lord to reveal to your mind every sexual use of your body as an instrument of unrighteousness. As the Lord brings them to your mind, renounce every sexual relationship you have had with another woman, and ask God to break that sexual and emotional bond. Your body belongs to God and it is not to be used for sexual immorality.

Third, present your body to God as a living sacrifice and reserve the sexual use of your body for your spouse only.

Finally, resist the devil, and he will flee from you.

Dan: I think I'm getting the picture. But every sexual use of my body! That will take a long time. Even if it takes a couple of hours, I guess it will be a lot easier than living in bondage for the rest of my life. I've been condemning myself for my inability to live the Christian life. I can also see why I have been questioning my salvation. Paul, though he was frustrated about his failure, didn't get down on himself. He accepted his responsibility. More important, he expressed confidence by turning to God, because the Lord Jesus Christ would enable him to live above sin.

Neil: You're on the right track. Condemning yourself won't help because there is no condemnation for those who are in Christ Jesus (Romans 8:1). We don't want to assist the devil in his role as the accuser. Most people who are in bondage question their salvation. I have counseled hundreds of people who have shared with me their doubts about God and themselves. Ironically, the very fact that they are sick of their sin and want to get out of it is one of the biggest assurances of their salvation. Non-Christians don't have those kinds of convictions.

There is one more important thing you need to know: No one particular sin, including sexual sin, is isolated from the rest of your life and the rest of reality. To gain complete freedom, you need to walk through all the Steps to Freedom in Christ. You also need to understand the battle that is going on for your mind, and that is what we will discuss next.

CHAPTER SEVEN

Winning the Battle for Your Mind

*The sins of the mind are
the last habitation of the devil.*

JAROL JOHNSON

SUPPOSE YOU HAVE WORKED MOST OF your adult life for the same boss—a cantankerous, unreasonable tyrant. The man is known throughout the company for bursting into employees' offices and verbally abusing them for even the slightest error or discrepancy. You learned early during your employment to walk silently around the old grouch and avoid him as much as possible. Every time he appears at your door, you cringe in fear.

One day you arrive at work to learn that the old tyrant has been transferred to another branch. You are no longer under his authority, and your relationship with him has ended. Your new boss is mild-mannered, kind, considerate, and affirming. He has the best interests of his employees at heart. But you don't know that at first, so when you see your new boss coming down the hall, you start looking for a place to hide, just like you did around the old boss. When he steps into your office, your heart starts beating faster. You wonder what you're going to get reamed out for this time. Over time you get to know your new boss a little better, and your response to him changes. But it will take time to get to know him and to change your attitudes and actions toward him.

Old habits are hard to break. The more we are conditioned to a certain stimulus–response pattern, the more difficult it is to reprogram our minds. This is certainly true of established sexual thought patterns and habits that are contrary to God's Word. For many people, these flesh patterns, or mental strongholds, have been ingrained in their minds since long before they became Christians.

Breaking the Strongholds Is Possible

Can strongholds of sexual bondage in the mind be broken? Yes! If our minds have been programmed wrongly, they can be reprogrammed. If we have been conformed to this world, we can be transformed. If we learned something the wrong way, we can learn it the right way. Will this take time? Yes, it will take the rest of our lives to renew our minds and to develop our character. We will never be perfect in our understanding on this earth, nor will our character be perfect like Christ's, but this is what we pursue.

Christian maturity cannot fully take place, however, unless Christians are firmly rooted in Christ. When people aren't experiencing their freedom in Christ they go from book to book, from pastor to pastor, and from counselor to counselor, but nothing seems to get resolved. Watch how fast they can grow, however, when they have genuinely repented and put their hope and trust in God.

After I had the privilege of helping a missionary find her freedom in Christ, she wrote,

> I'm firmly convinced of the significant benefits of finding our freedom in Christ. I was making some progress in therapy, but there is no comparison with the steps I am able to make now. My ability to "process" things has increased manyfold. Not only is my spirit more serene, my head is actually clearer! It's easier to

make connections now. It seems like everything is easier to understand now.

As we set about demolishing sexual strongholds in our mind, we are not just up against the world—the godless system we were raised in. And we are not just up against the flesh—including those preprogrammed habit patterns of thought that have been burned into our minds over time or by intense traumatic experiences. We're up against the world, the flesh, and the devil. All three influences are at work to turn our minds away from the truth and set us on a path to sexual bondage.

We still live in a fallen world. Television programs will never be totally cleaned up. Work places may display pornography, and people will use the Lord's name in vain. The world's influence is all around us. As Paul identified himself more with Christ and less with the world, he was able to say, "May I never boast except in the cross of our Lord Jesus Christ, through which the world has been crucified to me, and I to the world" (Galatians 6:14). We must consider ourselves dead to a world system which is in opposition to God's truth and sexual purity.

The flesh also remains with the Christian after salvation, but as we bond to Christ we also crucify the flesh. "Those who belong to Christ Jesus have crucified the flesh with its passions and desires. Since we live by the Spirit, let us keep in step with the Spirit" (Galatians 5:24-25). Satan still rules over this fallen world, but we are alive in Christ and dead to sin. When we resist the devil he will flee from us (James 4:7).

A Process of Adjustment

In chapter 5, we learned from Romans 6 that we are no longer under the authority of sin and Satan because our relationship with sin has been severed. We are new creatures in Christ (2 Corinthians 5:17). Old flesh patterns and habits don't automatically go away, however. They are still ingrained in our minds after salvation. Traumatic memories of abuse during childhood may still cause us to recoil in pain. We have a new boss—Jesus Christ—but having lived under the domination of sin and Satan, we must adjust to the freedom our new Master has provided for us.

In Romans 6, Paul instructed us to believe that our relationship with God has set us free from our relationship with sin and Satan (verses 1-11). Then he challenged us to present ourselves and our bodies to God as instruments of righteousness (verses 12-13; 12:1). Knowing and doing this makes possible the next instruction:

> Do not conform any longer to the pattern of this world, but be transformed by the renewing of your mind. Then you will be able to test and approve what God's will is—his good, pleasing and perfect will (Romans 12:2).

In summary, here is what we have learned so far about overcoming sexual strongholds:

1. We have to know and choose to believe our identity and position in Christ—that we are alive in Christ and dead to sin. We have to know the truth that sets us free. This is the essential foundation for Christian living, because no one can consistently live in a way that is inconsistent with what they believe about themselves and God. What we do doesn't determine who we are. Who we are and what we believe about God and ourselves determines what we do.

2. We have to repent of our sins. For sexual sins, that includes renouncing every sexual use of our bodies as instruments of unrighteousness and presenting them to God as instruments of righteousness. Genuine repentance is accomplished by submitting to God and resisting the devil, as we see in James 4:7. (In our ministry, we use the Steps to Freedom in Christ to accomplish this.)

3. We have to be transformed by the renewing of our minds.

Renewing Our Minds

In chapter 4, we noted that everything programmed into our memory banks before Christ is still there after salvation. Our brains recorded every experience we ever had, good and bad. Nobody pushed the clear button. The good news—literally, the gospel—is that we have all the resources we need to renew our minds. The Lord has sent us the Holy Spirit, who is the Spirit of truth (John 14:16-17), and He will guide us into all truth (John 16:13). Because we are alive in Christ, "we have the mind of Christ" (1 Corinthians 2:16). We have superior weapons to win the battle for our minds. Paul wrote,

> Though we live in the world, we do not wage war as the world does. The weapons we fight with are not the weapons of the world. On the contrary, they have divine power to demolish strongholds. We demolish arguments and every pretension that sets itself up against the knowledge of God, and we take captive every thought to make it obedient to Christ (2 Corinthians 10:3-5).

Paul is not talking about defensive armor. He is talking about battering-ram weaponry that tears down strongholds in our minds that have been raised up against the knowledge of God.

Practice Threshold Thinking

Paul tells us, "No temptation has seized you except what is common to man. And God is faithful; he will not let you be tempted beyond what you can bear. But when you are tempted, he will also provide a way out so that you can stand up under it" (1 Corinthians 10:13). If we are going to take the "way out" God has provided for us, we must avail ourselves of God's provision and change how we respond at the threshold of every sexually tempting thought. We must take those first thoughts captive and make them obedient to Christ. If we allow ourselves to ruminate on tempting thoughts, we will eventually act on them.

For example, suppose a man is struggling with lust. One night his wife asks him to go to the store for milk. When he gets into the car, he wonders which store he should go to. He knows of a local convenience store that has a display of pornographic magazines. He can also buy milk at a grocery store that's safe— it doesn't peddle smut. But the memory of the seductive photos he has ogled before at the convenience store gives rise to a tempting thought. The more he thinks about it, the harder it is to resist. When he pulls out of the driveway, he heads for the convenience store.

He has already lost the battle for his mind. The tempter is beckoning him: *Go ahead and take a peek—you know you want to. Everybody does it. You'll get away with it. Who would know?* On the way to the convenience store, all kinds of rationalizing thoughts cross his mind. He prays, *Lord, if You don't want me to look at the pornography, have my pastor be in the store buying milk, or close the store before I get there.* Since the store is open (do you know any convenience stores that ever close in the evening?) and since his pastor isn't there, he takes a look. Our minds have an incredible propensity to rationalize, which is why tempting thoughts must be stopped the moment we first encounter them.

But the man's stolen pleasure doesn't last. Even before he leaves the store, guilt and shame overwhelm him. The devil has changed his role from tempter to accuser: *You sicko. How can you call yourself a Christian? You're pathetic!* "Why did I do it?" he moans. He did it primarily because he ignored the way of escape God made available to him before he even pulled out of the driveway. He failed to take that initial thought captive and make it obedient to Christ. Rare is the person who can turn away from sin once the initial tempting thought has been embraced.

Understanding How We Function

To gain a better understanding of sexual temptation and mental strongholds, we need to know how our outer (material) body relates to our inner (immaterial) soul or spirit (2 Corinthians 4:16). Our brain is part of our physical body. Our mind is part of our soul. There is a fundamental difference between our brain and our mind. When we die physically, our soul is separated from our body and our brain returns to dust. We will be present with the Lord and in our right minds.

The material and immaterial function together as shown in the following diagram.

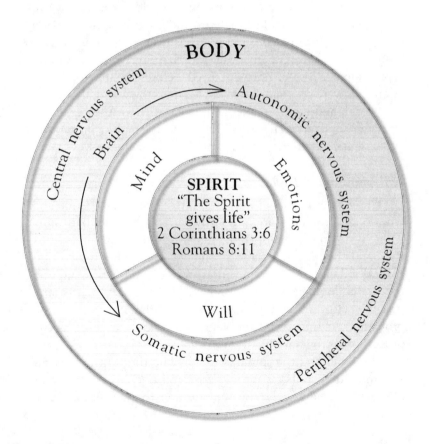

The primary correlation is between the mind and the brain. Our brain functions much like a digital computer. Neurons (brain cells) operate like little switches that turn on and off. Each neuron has many inputs—called dendrites—and only one output, which channels the neurotransmitters to dendrites of other neurons. Millions of these connections make up the hardware of our brain. There are approximately 40 different types of neurotransmitters, of which serotonin and dopamine are the ones we hear the most about. Only 5 percent of our neurotransmitters are in our brain—the rest are carrying signals throughout our body.

Our mind functions much like computer software. As our brain receives input from the external world through the five senses, our mind compiles, analyzes, and interprets the data and chooses responses based on how it has been programmed. Our brain can't function in any other way than in the way our mind is programmed. As we have discussed, before we came to Christ, our minds were programmed by inputs from the world, the god of this world, and by the choices we made without the benefit of knowing God and His ways. Every pornographic image and every sexual experience is still stored in our memories.

A Programming Problem

The Western medical world tends to assume that mental and emotional problems are primarily caused by the hardware. There is no doubt that organic brain syndrome, Alzheimer's disease, and chemical imbalances can affect our ability to function mentally. The best program (mind) won't work if the computer (brain) is unplugged or in disrepair. However, the Christian's struggle with sin and bondage is not primarily a hardware problem, but a software problem. Renewing our mind is the process of reprogramming the software.

The brain and the spinal cord make up the central nervous system, which splits off into a peripheral nervous system comprised of two channels: the somatic and the autonomic. The somatic nervous system regulates large and small muscular movements, over which we have volitional control. That is why we can consciously and volitionally move an arm, a leg, or a toe. The somatic nervous system obviously works together with our will. The autonomic system regulates our glands, over which we have no volitional control. We don't tell our heart to beat or our glands to secrete hormones into our bloodstream. The autonomic nervous system works together with our emotions, which we don't have volitional control over either. You cannot will yourself to change how you feel—but you can change how you think, which affects how you feel.

Sex glands are part of the autonomic nervous system. For instance, women have no volitional control over their menstrual cycles, and men have no volitional control over erections that occur during sleep. This is just the way God created our outer selves to operate.

If we have no control over our sex glands, then how can God expect us to have sexual self-control? Self-control is a fruit of the Spirit and a function of the inner self. Our sex glands are not the cause of sexual immorality; they just operate based on how our mind is programmed. Sexual behavior is determined by our thought life, and we *do* have control over what we think. If you fill your mind with pornography, you will drive your autonomic nervous system into the stops. Your sex glands will be set in motion, and you will likely behave in ways you will later regret. Just like a computer: If we put garbage in, we will get garbage out!

The Power of Visual Stimulation

Have you ever wondered why it is so hard to remember some things and to forget others? In school we study all night and then pray that the facts won't leave our mind before we take the big exam. One glance at a pornographic image, however, and it seems to stay in our mind for months and years. Why is that?

When we are stimulated emotionally—which includes being visually stimulated by sexual images—a signal is sent to our glands. A hormone called epinephrine is secreted into the bloodstream, which locks into our memory whatever stimulus is present at the time of the emotional excitement. This reaction causes us to involuntarily remember emotionally charged events—negative and traumatic ones as well as positive ones. It's too bad we don't get more emotionally excited about some of our subjects in school. We would remember them better!

It has been said that three viewings of hard-core pornography have the same lasting effect on us as the actual sexual experience. A person can become emotionally excited and sexually stimulated just from entertaining sexual thoughts. That's why an aroused man or woman will experience an emotional rush before any sexual contact is made. The man going to the convenience store where they sold pornography was sexually stimulated long before he even saw the magazines. The process begins in our thoughts, which trigger our autonomic nervous system, which secretes epinephrine into our bloodstream, which loads the image in our memory.

Emotions Are Products of Our Thoughts

Just as we can't volitionally control our glands, we can't directly control our emotions. If you think you can, try liking someone right now who you don't like! We can't command our emotions that way, nor are there any instructions in Scripture for us to do so. We must acknowledge our emotions, however, because we can't be right with God if we aren't real about how we feel. Though we can't tell ourselves not to feel a certain way and can only acknowledge or deny how we feel, we do have control over how we think—and how we think controls how we feel. Scripture *does* tell us to control our thinking: "Brothers, stop thinking like children. In regard to evil be infants, but in your thinking be adults" (1 Corinthians 14:20).

This line of reasoning is the basis for cognitive therapy. People are doing what they are doing and are feeling what they are feeling because of what they have chosen to think or believe. Therefore, we should try to change what we think or believe if we want to change our behavior or feelings. When applied from a Christian perspective, cognitive therapy is very close to repentance—which literally means "a change of mind."

If what we choose to believe does not reflect truth, then what we feel will not conform to reality. Let me illustrate. Suppose a man has been working for many years at a company that is now downsizing. People are getting laid off, but he thinks he is secure. Then one Monday morning he gets a note from his boss, telling him that his boss wants to see him the coming Friday at 10:30 A.M. At first he thinks it is nothing to be worried about...but he may be in denial. Then he begins to think he is going to get laid off, and he gets angry. *How could they lay me off? I have been a faithful employee for years. I am not going to give them the satisfaction. I'm going to see my boss this Wednesday and quit.* But he doesn't because his wife threatens to leave him if he does something so foolish.

Well, maybe they aren't going to lay me off, he reasons. Now he is double-minded and anxious. By Thursday afternoon, he is sure they are going to lay him off, and he is depressed. *How am I going to pay my bills, and Mary's college education?* By Friday morning he is an emotional basket case. He has experienced anger, anxiety, and depression because of the way he has thought, and not one of his feelings has conformed to reality...because the boss only wanted to give him a raise.

The Outcome of Wrong Sexual Thoughts

Our society seems to be ignorant of what sexual and violent impressions can do to our minds. This is illustrated by the concept of "adults only." The phrase implies there are separate standards of morality for adults and children. Television programs announce, "The following content is suitable for 'mature' audiences only. Viewer discretion is advised." The content isn't suitable for anyone, and mature people should be the first to know that. Adults should be mature enough to not allow their minds to be programmed with filth. In regard to evil, we should all be like infants: restricting ourselves only to wholesome entertainment. We have already been advised by God concerning sexual immorality in any form: "Flee" (1 Corinthians 6:18).

Since we have no control over how we feel, drop the following line from your repertoire, whether you use it in reference to yourself or to others: "You shouldn't feel that way." That's a subtle form of rejection, because we can't change how we feel. The point we have been making is that our feelings are primarily a product of our thought life. What we believe, how we think, and how we perceive ourselves and the world around us determines how we feel. The following story reinforces this concept.

Suppose you are paddling a canoe down a beautiful river in the wilderness enjoying God's creation. As you round a bend in the river, your serenity is disturbed. Standing on the riverbank is someone of the opposite sex. The person appears to be very attractive physically and beckons you toward the shore. There is a blanket spread on the bank, and your mind and emotions suddenly go wild with tempting possibilities. Your heart races and your palms are moist. *What an enticing opportunity. We're all alone out here. I can get away with this.* Ignoring your convictions, you paddle toward the shore with your emotions reading 9 on a scale of 1 to 10.

But as you draw nearer the shore, you see distress instead of seductiveness in the person's face—and you notice small sores, revealing that the person may be suffering from AIDS. You suddenly realize your initial impression of the stranger was all wrong, and your emotions quickly drop to a 1—from sexual arousal to revulsion, fear, and finally compassion for a person in need. You had a totally wrong perception, but your feelings responded to what you wanted to believe. It's clear the person wasn't beckoning you to the shore for a romantic interlude, but was calling for help after getting into trouble because of poor health. You confess to God your wrong thoughts and desires, and then you assist the person.

Your first thoughts about the person were wrong—therefore what you felt was a distortion of reality. If what we see or mentally visualize is morally wrong, then our emotions are going to be bound to the wrong stimulus. That is why true romantic Christian love is associated with love and trust, but sexual immorality is often tied into fear and danger. It is actually *eros,* or erotic love, rather than *agape* love. If you want to feel right, you must think right.

Check for Viruses

Reprogramming our minds is the path to maturity, but we had better check for viruses. Paul writes, "The Spirit clearly says that in later times some will abandon the faith and follow deceiving spirits and things taught by demons" (1 Timothy 4:1). I have counseled hundreds of people who struggle with their thoughts or literally hear "voices." In most cases, the root problem has proven to be a spiritual battle for their minds.

If Satan can get us to believe a lie, he can control our lives. He is intent on destroying a proper perception of God, ourselves, members of the opposite sex—including our spouses—and the world we live in. Our problems don't just stem from what we have believed in the past. Paul says we are to presently and continuously take every thought captive and make it obedient to Christ (2 Corinthians 10:5).

Unforgiveness

The word "thought" in the above verse is the Greek word *noema.* Notice the topic Paul is addressing when he uses this word elsewhere in 2 Corinthians: "I have forgiven in the sight of Christ for your sake, in order that Satan might not outwit us.

For we are not unaware of his schemes [noema]" (2:10-11). Nothing will keep us in bondage to our past more than unforgiveness. God Himself will turn us over to the "torturers" if we don't forgive others from our hearts (Matthew 18:34 NASB), because He doesn't want us chained to the past. I believe the greatest access Satan has to the church is our unwillingness to forgive those who have offended us. This has certainly been true of the thousands of people I have been privileged to work with.

If you have been sexually abused, you have probably struggled with thoughts like "I can't forgive that person," "I hate that person," or "I don't want to forgive him, I want him to suffer as much as he made me suffer." Satan is probably tormenting you. "But you don't know how bad the person hurt me," you say. They are still hurting you.

Forgiveness, however, is the means by which we set ourselves free from abusers. We are to forgive as Christ has forgiven us. He did that by taking upon Himself the consequences for our sins. When we choose to forgive others, we are agreeing to live with the consequences of their sins. "That's not fair!" you say as an abused person. True, but you will have to live with the consequences anyway. The only real choice is whether you do it in the bondage of bitterness or the freedom of forgiveness. "Where is the justice?" you ask. It is in the cross. Jesus died once for all our sins. "But why should I let the abuser off my hook?" That is why you forgive—so that you are no longer hooked to them. They are not off God's hook, though—revenge is His, and there will be a final judgment.

Lies from Satan

Look at another passage in 2 Corinthians: "The god of this age [Satan] has blinded the minds [noema] of unbelievers, so that they cannot see the light of the gospel of the glory of Christ" (4:4). The one who raises up thoughts against the knowledge of God has a field day with the sexually abused. "Where is your God now?" he taunts. "If God is love, why does He allow the innocent to suffer? If God is all-powerful, why didn't He stop that person from violating you?" The lies of Satan have blinded many people to the truth.

Consider one more verse: "I am afraid that just as Eve was deceived by the serpent's cunning, your minds [noema] may somehow be led astray from your sincere and pure devotion to Christ" (2 Corinthians 11:3). I'm concerned too, because I see so many people living in bondage to the serpent's lies, which draws them away from their devotion to Christ.

Satan is the father of lies, and he will work on our minds to destroy our concept of God and our understanding of who we are as children of God. People in bondage don't know who they are in Christ. That is the one common denominator in every person I have been privileged to help find freedom in Christ. Satan can't do anything about our position in Christ—but if he can get us to believe it isn't true, we will live as though it isn't.

Satan's Targets

Satan preys on the minds of wounded people—the victims of broken marriages, the children of alcoholics, and those who were sexually abused as children. They are prime candidates for Satan's lies because their minds have already been pummeled by self-doubt, fear, anger, and hatred because of their abuse. But you don't have to be the victim of a broken home or a painful childhood to be the target of the enemy's temptations, accusations, and deceptions.

For example, suppose in a vulnerable moment a young woman has a tempting sexual thought toward another woman. At first she can't believe she could be tempted to homosexuality. She is embarrassed and immediately flees from the tempting situation. But she decides not to tell anyone about it. Who would understand? Then when it happens again and again, she begins to wonder, *Why am I thinking like this? Is there something wrong with me? Could I be one of them?* Now that the door of doubt is open, she begins to seriously question her sexuality.

If her mind continues to dwell on those tempting thoughts, it will affect the way she feels. That's the way God made us. If she believes what she feels and behaves accordingly, she will use her body as an instrument of unrighteousness and sin will reign in her mortal body. To resolve this, she must renounce that sexual use of her body with any other person, renounce the lie that she is homosexual, and renew her mind with the truth of God's Word.

While I was speaking at a camp, a mother called and asked if she and her twelve-year-old son could spend an hour with me. The husband couldn't come, though he wanted to. This was a very close family of three. The young boy was a leader at school and church, but one Sunday he had been overwhelmed by homosexual thoughts toward the pastor. The boy had such a good relationship with his parents that he had told them about it. That was highly unusual, and it was just as unusual that the parents knew what to do about it. They had recognized where those thoughts were coming from. They had just instructed their son not to pay any attention to them and to keep affirming the truth, which he did. By the time we met, the thoughts were completely gone. Had he not told his parents, he probably would have thought something was terribly wrong with him, and eventually acted on his impulses—and the whole family would have been torn up.

Don't assume that all disturbing thoughts are from Satan. We live in a sinful world with tempting images and messages all around us. You have memories of hurtful experiences, which prompt thoughts contrary to the knowledge of God. Whether a thought is introduced into your mind from the television set, your memory bank, the pit of hell, or your own imagination doesn't matter in one sense, because we are instructed to take *every* thought captive in obedience to Christ. If it isn't true, don't think or believe it.

You can try to analyze the source of every thought, but it won't resolve the problem. Too much of the recovery movement is caught up in the paralysis of analysis—and even a perfect analysis of the problem doesn't bring relief. The answer is a personal relationship with Christ. His truth will set us free if we believe it. We will experience this freedom and His presence if we repent.

Cleaning Up the Mind
by Choosing the Truth

If you deal with tempting thoughts by trying to rebuke every negative thought, it won't work. You will be like the person in the middle of a lake treading water and trying to keep 12 corks submerged. You knock one down, another comes up. You should ignore the stupid corks and swim to shore. As believers, we are not called to dispel the darkness, we are called to turn on the light. We overcome negative thoughts by choosing the truth. "Finally, brothers, whatever is true, whatever is noble, whatever is right, whatever is pure, whatever is lovely, whatever is admirable—if anything is excellent or praiseworthy—think about such things" (Philippians 4:8).

The next verse says we must also put it into practice. We speak the truth in love. We do the noble, right, pure, and lovely thing. Those who only hear the word and don't do it are deluded, according to James 1:22. We can do these things if we have genuinely repented by submitting to God and resisting the devil. Those who are experiencing their freedom in Christ can process new truth and grow in Him. Those who haven't fully repented are bopping down corks. They are barely surviving as they tread water in the cesspool of life.

Paul wanted to give the church at Corinth solid food, but he couldn't because they were not able to receive it (1 Corinthians 3:2). So he could give them only milk. They weren't able to receive it, because of the jealousy and strife among them (verse 3). If there were no way to resolve the personal problems people are having, then there would be no way for them to grow. The good news is, we can resolve our personal and spiritual conflicts through genuine repentance and faith in God.

When I was a young Christian, I decided to clean up my mind. I had had a good upbringing, for which I am thankful, and had become a Christian in my twenties. After four years in the Navy, however, my mind was polluted with a lot of junk. I had seen enough pornography aboard ship to plague me for years. Images would dance in my mind for months after one look. I hated it. I struggled every time I went to a place where pornography was available.

When I made the decision to clean up my mind, do you think the battle got easier or harder? It got harder, of course. Temptation isn't much of a battle if you easily give in to it. It is fierce when you decide to stand against it. I finally got the victory, however. The following illustration may be helpful as you set out to rid your mind of years of impure thoughts.

Think of your polluted mind as a pot filled to the brim with stale black coffee. It is dark and smelly. There is no way to get the pollution of coffee out of the liquid. However, sitting beside the coffeepot is a huge bowl of crystal-clear ice, which represents the Word of God. Your goal is to purify the contents of the pot by adding ice cubes to it every day. I wish there were a way to dump all the cubes (words of the Bible) in at one time, but there isn't. Every cube dilutes the mixture, though, making it a little purer. You can only put in one or two cubes a day, so the process seems futile at first. But over the course of time, the water begins to look less and less polluted, and the taste and smell of coffee decreases. The process continues to work provided you don't add more coffee grounds. If you read your Bible then look at pornography, you are treading water at best.

Paul writes, "Let the peace of Christ rule in your hearts, since as members of one body you were called to peace. And be thankful" (Colossians 3:15). How do we rid ourselves of evil thoughts, purify our mind, and allow the peace of Christ to reign? The answer is found in Colossians 3:16: "Let the word of

Christ dwell in you richly." The psalmist gives similar instruction: "How can a young man keep his way pure? By living according to your word. I seek you with all my heart; do not let me stray from your commands. I have hidden your word in my heart that I might not sin against you" (Psalm 119:9-11). Merely trying to stop thinking bad thoughts won't work. We must fill our minds with the crystal-clear Word of God. There is no alternative plan. We overcome the father of lies by choosing the truth!

A Winnable Battle

You may find that winning the battle for your mind will initially be two steps forward, and one step back. Gradually it will become three steps forward, and one step back, then four and five steps forward as you learn to take every thought captive and make it obedient to Christ. You may despair with all your steps backward, but God won't give up on you. Remember, your sins are already forgiven. This is a winnable battle, because you are alive in Christ and dead to sin. The bigger war has already been won by Christ.

Freedom to be all that God has called you to be is the greatest blessing in this present life. This freedom is worth fighting for. As you learn more about who you are as a child of God and about the nature of the battle waging for your mind, the process becomes easier. Eventually it is 20 steps forward and one back, and finally the steps are all forward, with only an occasional slip in the battle for the mind.

CHAPTER EIGHT

Recovery in Christ

*When I nominated Jesus as my supreme ecologist,
years of inner pollution became instantly
biodegradable.*

DONALD R. BROWN

NANCY, A DEVOTED WIFE AND MOTHER, attended our "Living Free in Christ" conference. During the sessions I related several stories of persons who had experienced abuse and found their freedom in Christ. As Nancy listened to the testimonies she felt nauseated, dizzy, and disgusted. Later in the week she confronted me with stern questions: "Why are you telling these awful stories? Those poor children were not at fault. I'm so angry with you. Why are you doing this?"

I wasn't surprised by Nancy's response, because the conference often brings to light in people a lot of problems that haven't been dealt with. I told her, "These stories are not intended to cause pain—they are stories of victory and hope. I don't think your response has anything to do with me or the testimonies. The Lord is using this conference to bring to the surface something in your life that hasn't been resolved, and the evil one doesn't like it. He's behind your agitation. Please talk with one of our Freedom in Christ staff members, who can arrange a freedom appointment for you." Nancy spent the rest of that morning and part of the afternoon finding her freedom in Christ.

Two weeks later Nancy shared her testimony with me, which related to a bedtime story she had often read to her children, *The Bears on Hemlock Mountain.* She recounted how Jonathan, the main character in the story, trudged up the mountain to fetch a large kettle for his mother. On the way he sang, "There are no bears on Hemlock Mountain. No bears. No bears. No bears at all."

He saw dark figures in the distance that looked like bears. But he knew they couldn't be bears, because he didn't want to believe there were bears on Hemlock Mountain. So he continued to climb and sing, "There are no bears on Hemlock Mountain. No bears. No bears. No bears at all." Then he saw a bear. He quickly scrambled under the kettle for safety. He remained hidden until his father and uncles arrived with their guns to rescue him from the bears.

Nancy said that she had been confronted with a "dark figure" from her past, but she had not allowed her mind to accept the possibility that there were bears on her mountain of pain: "There was no sexual molestation in my past, no sexual molestation at all." But there were "bear tracks" everywhere. Memories of sexual abuse flooded her mind, but she didn't want to admit it and face the truth. She had hidden under a kettle of denial until she hadn't been able to anymore.

During the conference, she had understood that she no longer needed to be afraid because her heavenly Father had overcome the painful threat of the bear of sexual abuse. He had already destroyed the bear—and facing the truth was her only way to get off the mountain. After she had renounced the unrighteous use of her body and forgiven her abuser, there was peace in her life and safety at last on "Hemlock Mountain."

Perhaps your experience parallels that of Nancy. The truth and testimonies in the previous chapters of this book have brought into sharp focus your shame, failure, and pain in the area of sexual promiscuity, sexual disorientation, or sexual abuse. You may have been in denial for years, insisting, "I don't have a problem." But your lack of peace and victory regarding the sexual sin in your life has worn you down. Try as you might to avoid it, you keep falling into the same thoughts and behaviors again and again. You're too tired to run away anymore. You're ready to throw off the chains of sexual bondage, as made possible by Christ.

As I have indicated throughout this book, finding your freedom in Christ comes through knowing and believing the truth, followed by genuine repentance. We use the Steps to Freedom in Christ in our ministry to guide Christians through a repentance process of submitting to God and resisting the devil (James 4:7).*

Take the Initiative

A prerequisite to finding your freedom from sexual bondage is to face the truth, acknowledge the problem, and assume responsibility to change. You are responsible for confessing and repenting of your own sin. No one can do that for you. Inherent in this process is your willingness to submit to God completely without trying to hide anything from Him. Adam and Eve were created to live in a transparent relationship with God. They walked with God daily in the garden, naked and unashamed. When they sinned, Adam and Eve covered their nakedness and tried to avoid God. It is foolish to try hiding from an all-knowing God. We mistakenly think that if we go about our daily business, God won't see us hiding in the darkness. We must give up our defensive, self-protective posture and walk in the light of His presence.

Repentance means to have a change of mind. It is far more than just mental acknowledgment, however. It means to turn

---

* The theology and process of the Steps is explained in *Discipleship Counseling* (Regal Books, 2003). The *Steps to Freedom in Christ* (Regal Books, 2000) can be purchased in book form at any Christian bookstore or from Freedom in Christ Ministries. They are also included in *The Bondage Breaker* (Harvest House Publishers, 2000).

from our self-centered and self-indulging ways and trust in God. It means to no longer hold iniquity in our hearts. Repentance involves not only what we turn *from* but who we turn *to*. We must commit all we have and all we are to God. We are to be faithful stewards of everything that God has entrusted to us (1 Corinthians 4:1-2). Such a commitment should include our possessions, our ministries, our families, our minds, and our physical bodies. We should renounce any previous use of our lives and possessions in the service of sin and then dedicate ourselves to the Lord. In so doing, we are saying that the god of this world no longer has any right over us because we belong to God.

Taking Steps to Reclaim Your Heritage

At this point, I urge you to obtain a copy of the Steps to Freedom in Christ. They were developed to assist us as believers to resolve our personal and spiritual conflicts. In so doing, we claim the freedom that was purchased on the cross and fully deeded over to us by the resurrected Christ. The Steps cover seven critical areas affecting our relationship with God, areas where you may have allowed the prince of darkness to establish strongholds in your life. God has done everything necessary to set you free. It is your responsibility to appropriate what He has done and then to stand firm and resist the evil one.

How you view the experience will greatly determine what you gain from it. If you see the Steps as a means to rid yourself of bad habits—like employing a counseling technique to move from one life-stage to another—you will receive only limited benefits. This process is an encounter with God. There is nothing magical about going through it. The Steps do not set people free—Jesus does. Jesus is the Bondage Breaker and the only One who can set you free. Establishing your freedom in Him is dependent upon your response to God in repentance and faith.

You can go through the process on your own, but you will find great benefit in going through the Steps in one sitting with a mature Christian friend or leader who can provide accountability and objectivity. Allow plenty of time for the process. It may require several hours to break through the spiritual strongholds that have been erected in your life.

Important Steps for Sexual Victims

There are two of the Steps that are crucial for you to process if you have been victimized by rape, incest, or other forms of sexual abuse. Because of their importance, both of these issues have been mentioned previously in this book. The first is forgiving those who have offended you, and the second is breaking the sexual and emotional bonds that were formed when you were violated.

A Choice for Freedom

Forgiveness can be the most difficult step for anyone who has suffered severely at the hands of a sexual offender. As difficult as it may be, forgiving your offender actually sets you free from their offense. Forgiveness is a choice, an act of your will. You must choose to forgive for your own sake. It is the only way to be free of the bitterness that may have filled your heart.

As you process this step, Satan may try to convince you that forgiving the offender somehow makes what he or she did right. That's a lie. What the offender did to you can never be justified. You were stripped of your safety and used for someone else's pleasure. That person owes you a debt that can never be paid. The wrongs of the past do not become right when you forgive—but by forgiving you can be free of them.

In forgiving, you must relinquish your anger, which may have been used as a defense against other violations. Your anger is a signal that you have been threatened or hurt, and a motivation to take action. The proper action to take is to forgive and then set up scriptural boundaries so the offender cannot hurt you again. When you deal with the offense, the anger will dissipate. When you choose to forgive by facing all your painful memories—the hate, the hurt, the absolute ugliness of what the offender did to you—you will be free. (Step 3 will guide you through this important process.)

Breaking Unrighteous Bonds

Another vital step to gaining freedom from past offenses is to ask God to break the spiritual bonds that were formed when you were violated sexually. When a husband and wife consummate their marriage physically, they become one. A physical, emotional, and spiritual bond is formed. When your body was used for unrighteous sexual purposes, a bond was formed—not the holy bond God ordained for marriage, but an unholy bond. You may have been an unwitting or unwilling participant in this union, but a bond was formed nevertheless.

I have learned through much experience to encourage sexual abuse victims to ask the Lord to reveal every sexual use of their body as an instrument of unrighteousness. Once the experiences are brought to light and renounced, the bondage is broken. (Step 6 will guide you through the process of breaking sexual bonds with abusers.)

Beth had been sexually abused. Her behavior was tearing up her parents and destroying their Christian home. Usually nothing good comes from appointments made by parents for children who don't want to be helped, but Beth's parents assured me that she wanted to see me.

Her opening statement was, "I don't want to get right with God or anything like that!" I have learned that such statements are just a dodge, and I don't let them discourage me. I said, "I am willing to accept your choices. But since you're here, maybe you could share with me how you have been hurt." She told me the story of being date-raped by the campus hero at her high school. At the time she was too embarrassed to tell anyone about it, and she had no idea how to resolve it. Having lost her virginity, she became sexually promiscuous, living off and on with an immoral man.

I asked Beth's permission to lead her through the Steps, and she agreed. When I invited her to ask the Lord to reveal to her mind every sexual use of her body as an instrument of unrighteousness, she said, "That would be embarrassing!" So I stepped out of the room while a female prayer partner helped her through the process. That night she was singing in church for the first time in years. She was experiencing her freedom.

A New Beginning

The Steps to Freedom in Christ are not an end in themselves. They offer a new beginning. For some people, the first time through the Steps will represent the first major victory in a war that continues on. The following testimony is from a man who was formerly trapped in nearly every form of sexual bondage mentioned in this book. It illustrates the process of securing freedom in Christ one victory at a time.

> My dad left our home when I was four years old. Every day I cried out to God to bring my daddy home. But he never came back. So my mother, my brother, and I moved in with my grandparents. I disconnected from God early in life because no one tried to explain why He never answered my pleas.
>
> One night my grandfather undressed in front of me and my grandmother. He had an erection. Although he wouldn't have done anything to hurt me, my grandfather's act of indiscretion left a terrible mark in my mind that surfaced years later.
>
> In the absence of my father, as a young boy I bonded with my grandfather. I thought he loved me. It didn't matter to me that he had been unfaithful to my grandmother, had sexually abused my mother, and was becoming an alcoholic. When my mother remarried and we moved away, I felt like I had lost my father for a second time. But I didn't bother to ask God for help, because I felt He had let me down.

We moved every year as I grew up. Every time I made a friend, we moved again, keeping the wounds of abandonment and loneliness painful. I grieved over every loss and did everything to protect myself from being hurt again.

I believed I was different from most boys. I started playing sexually with some of my male friends during grade school. Voices in my head told me it was okay because I was born that way. I had a terrible male void in my life, and my heart burned with desire. The memory of seeing my grandfather with an erection prompted a fascination with seeing boys and men naked. Voyeurism became a way of life for me.

Meanwhile, my own family was being ripped apart by conflict. The squabbles and fights mortified me. I was a loyal and sensitive kid who carried a deep concern for everyone in my family. I tried to convince my friends' parents to adopt me in order to escape the turmoil, but it didn't work. I finally detached completely from my mother and brother.

As an adolescent and young adult, I threw myself into the gay world. I was addicted to watching men in public restrooms, and I visited gay bars almost every night. When I found a gay lover, I thought I had finally met a man who would love me and stay with me forever. I was emotionally codependent on him. When the relationship ended after three years, I fell into a deep depression. I was emotionally bankrupt and lost. News of my brother's death added to my sense of despair and abandonment.

At his funeral I purchased a Bible, but I didn't know why. I kept it on my nightstand with a cross someone had given me. I didn't dare move them. I was terrified every night, feeling a horrifying dark presence around me. Someone told me to hold the cross and yell, "I bind you in the name of Jesus Christ of Nazareth." I did so night after night with the covers pulled up to my neck. But something kept tormenting me.

I finally started reading the Bible and attending church. I accepted the Lord at a baptism service and left the gay lifestyle

completely. I studied the Word seriously, but with my back-
ground it was easy to fall into legalism. I didn't understand grace
and forgiveness. The Bible talked a lot about sexual immorality
and clearly forbade homosexual behavior. I asked myself, *If I am
a Christian, why do I still feel the same homosexual tendencies?*
The more I tried to do what the Bible said and what others
expected of me, the more guilty I felt. I didn't dare tell anyone
what I was feeling. The voyeurism became intense and triggered
an uncontrollable bondage to masturbation.

When I began teaching a Sunday school class, the voices in
my head condemned me daily and accused me of being a hypocrite. I believed them. I was tormented. The more I fought
back by reading my Bible and serving the Lord, the greater the
oppression became. My mind was ruled by immoral thoughts. I
experienced intense sexual dreams. I was out of control and
backsliding quickly. I found myself back in public restrooms. I
talked to Christian counselors and pastors, but no one seemed
to be able to offer a workable solution to my problem. I wanted
so badly to know and serve the Lord.

A friend who was aware of my struggle gave me a copy of *Victory over the Darkness* by Neil Anderson. As I began reading it, the
book seemed to be written about me. For the first time I understood how I had gotten into my horrible condition and how I
could get out of it. No one had ever told me I was a child of
God, that God had chosen me as His friend, and that He loved
me specifically. I had learned about God intellectually, but
through reading this book I finally met my gentle and loving
heavenly Father personally.

When I read *The Bondage Breaker,* I knew I was spiritually
oppressed. I had been involved in almost everything in the non-
Christian spiritual experience inventory at the end of the book.
I began to understand my oppressive thought life, rampant
voyeurism, and low sense of worth. I discovered that realizing I am
a child of God was the answer to breaking the destructive cycle
that had been present in my family for generations.

I learned that Jesus is the Bondage Breaker and that I have authority over the kingdom of darkness because I am seated with Christ in the heavenlies. However, the more I embraced these truths, the more I was attacked. I was falling apart emotionally. I had to see Neil Anderson.

I attended one of his conferences and my entire life was changed. One of his staff met with me in a four-hour session. No one had ever wanted to spend that much time with me. I felt free for the first time in my life. Still, my desperate need for affirmation prevented me from being totally honest in the counseling session.

Two days later Neil talked about forgiving others. I asked him if a person has to cry when they forgive someone. He didn't answer. He made me think about it. On the way back to my motel, I told the Lord I really wanted to forgive my dad and stepdad for not validating me. Then the Lord let me feel the pain of not being validated. He gave me a glimpse of His pain on the cross. I cried so hard I could hardly drive. Then I thought of the women in my life that had hurt me so badly. The floodgates opened as I forgave each person from my heart.

I was free, but Neil shared with me that people who have been in bondage a long time are more like onions than bananas. You peel a banana once, and that's it. But an onion has many layers. He cautioned me that I had successfully worked through at least one layer of my problem. Other layers might surface, but at least I knew how to respond when they did.

After a couple of months, the glow of my freedom subsided. I started to backslide and return to voyeurism. I read Neil's books *Released from Bondage* and *Finding God's Will in Spiritually Deceptive Times*. I fought back against the attack and worked through the issues. Another layer of the onion was peeled away. I felt renewed again, but also worn out from the battle. I wasn't reading the Word or praying much. I didn't feel like doing it.

So I started reading Neil and Joanne's devotional, *Daily in Christ*. I was filled with guilt because of my mental lapses into voyeurism and masturbation. How could I teach Sunday school and be such a hypocrite? I told the Lord I really loved Him and wanted to serve Him. Then I decided to prove it. I had always been fearful of vows, but I made one. I told the Lord I was His child and I was going to be baptized again. I knew that I didn't have to and that baptism didn't save me, but I wanted to erect a milestone for the Lord like the Israelites did when they crossed the Jordan.

I made the vow, and the Lord honored it beyond my wildest anticipation. He confirmed in me that I was a child of God and that He loved me. Once I submitted myself completely to Him and stopped trying to fix myself, He was able to do it for me.

The masturbation stopped instantaneously and has never come back. The voyeurism has also stopped. I have learned what it means to take every thought captive in obedience to Christ. Now I measure everything that comes into my mind against what the Lord says in His Word, and the truth has set me free.

Now that I know I am a child of God, there is no more low self-worth, inferiority, obsessive, negative, or perverse thoughts, or secret behavior. I busted through that last layer of the onion like a rocket. There may be more layers ahead, but this time I am armed with the Lord's belt of truth.

Maintaining Your Freedom

Your experience of repentance by going through the Steps to Freedom in Christ may be different from the experiences of others. Each individual is unique, and each has his or her unique set of conflicts to resolve. Some people are elated by the overwhelming sense of peace they feel for the very first time. Others may have to work through many layers. If you have repressed memories, I have found that God will graciously reveal them one layer at a time—probably because we couldn't handle doing it all at once.

Paul wrote, "It is for freedom that Christ has set us free" (Galatians 5:1). Once we have tasted freedom in Christ, we must maintain our relationship with God by continuing to stand in the truth of His Word. Paul completes the verse by encouraging us: "Stand firm, then, and do not let yourselves be burdened again by a yoke of slavery." Freedom is our inheritance, but we must not turn our freedom into ritualistic rules and regulations, which is legalism, or an opportunity to indulge our fleshly nature, which is license (Galatians 5:13). The steps you take to experience your freedom in Christ are not the end of the journey but the beginning of a walk in the Spirit. Therefore, I say with Paul in Galatians 5:16,

Walk by the Spirit, and you will not
carry out the desire of the flesh.

1. According to an editorial by Pulitzer prize–winning cartoonist Steve Benson in the June 24, 2003, edition of the *Arizona Republic*. He further stated, "The battle is over, gays have won." In the August 6, 2003, edition of the same paper, it was reported that the Episcopal Church of the USA has confirmed its first openly homosexual bishop, Gene Robinson, who left his wife and family to live with another man.

2. Centers for Disease Control and Prevention, *Tracking the Hidden Epidemics: Trends in STDs in the United States* (2000), p. 1. Accessed via Internet at www.cdc.gov/nchstp/dstd/Stats_Trends/Trends2000.pdf.

3. S.J. De Vries, "Sin, sinners," G. Buttrick et al., *Interpreter's Dictionary of the Bible*, vol. 4 (Nashville, TN: Abingdon, 1962), p. 365.

4. De Vries, p. 366. De Vries comes to his conclusion based on the following: "The corporate involvement of sin deeply impressed itself upon the people...The prophets proclaimed that it was not only a few wicked individuals, but the whole nation, that was laden with sin (see Isaiah 1:4). Generation upon generation treasured up wrath. Thus it was easy for those who were finally forced to bear the painful consequences to protest that all the effects of corporate guilt were being visited upon them. The exiles lamented: 'Our fathers sinned, and are no more; it is we who have borne their iniquities' (Lamentations 5:7). They even had a proverb: 'The fathers have eaten sour grapes, and the children's teeth are set on edge.' Against this both Jeremiah and Ezekiel protested (see Jeremiah 31:29,30; Ezekiel 18; 33:10-20). No son was to be held accountable for his father's crimes. 'The soul that sins shall die' (Ezekiel 18:4)." (De Vries, pp. 365-366)

5. Maxine Hancock and Karen Burton-Mains, *Child Sexual Abuse: A Hope for Healing* (Wheaton, IL: Harold Shaw Publishers, 1987), p. 12.

6. Herant A. Katchadourian and Donald T. Lunde, *Fundamentals of Human Sexuality*, 3rd ed. (New York: Holt, Rinehart, and Winston Publishers, 1987), p. 379.

7. Adapted from Neil T. Anderson, *The Bondage Breaker* (Eugene, OR: Harvest House Publishers, 2000), pp. 53-57.

Books and Resources from Freedom in Christ Ministries and Neil T. Anderson

Core Message and Resources

- *The Bondage Breaker*® (Harvest House). Study guide and audiobook also available. This book explains spiritual warfare, what your protection is, ways that you are vulnerable, and how you can live a liberated life in Christ. Well over one million copies in print.

- *Victory Over the Darkness* with study guide, audio book, and videos (Regal Books). Explains who you are in Christ, how you walk by faith, how your mind and emotions function, and how to relate to one another in Christ. Well over one million copies in print.

- *Breaking Through to Spiritual Maturity* (Regal Books). A curriculum for teaching the basic message of Freedom in Christ Ministries.

- *Discipleship Counseling* with videos (Regal Books). Discipleship and counseling are integrated practically with theology and psychology to help Christians resolve personal and spiritual conflicts through repentance.

- *Steps to Freedom in Christ* and interactive video (Regal Books). This discipleship counseling tool helps Christians resolve their personal and spiritual conflicts.

The Bondage Breaker® Series (Harvest House). Truth from the Word of God on specific issues—to bring you help and freedom in your life.

- *Praying by the Power of the Spirit*
- *Finding God's Will in Spiritually Deceptive Times*
- *Finding Freedom in a Sex-Obsessed World*

Resources on Specific Issues

- *Getting Anger Under Control* with Rich Miller (Harvest House). Exposes the basis for anger and shows how you can control it.

- *Freedom from Fear* with Rich Miller (Harvest House). Discusses fear, anxiety, and anxiety disorders and reveals how you can be free from them.

- *Daily in Christ* (Harvest House). This popular daily devotional will encourage, motivate, and challenge you to experience the reality of *Christ in you.*

- *Breaking the Bondage of Legalism* with Rich Miller and Paul Travis (Harvest House). An exposure and explanation of legalism, the guilt and shame it brings, and how you can overcome it.

- *God's Power at Work in You* with Dr. Robert Saucy (Harvest House). A thorough analysis of sanctification, along with practical instruction on how you can grow in Christ.

- *A Way of Escape* (Harvest House). Exposes the bondage of sexual strongholds and shows you how they can be torn down in Christ.

- *The Seduction of Our Children* with Steve Russo (Harvest House). Reveals what teenagers are experiencing and how you as a parent can be equipped to help them.

- *Who I Am in Christ* (Regal Books). Thirty-six short chapters on who you are in Christ and how He meets your deepest needs.

- *Freedom from Addiction* with Mike Quarles (Regal Books).

- *One Day at a Time* with Mike Quarles (Regal Books).

- *The Christ-Centered Marriage* with Dr. Charles Mylander (Regal Books).

- *The Spiritual Protection of Our Children* with Peter and Sue Vander Hook (Regal Books).

- *Leading Teens to Freedom in Christ* with Rich Miller (Regal Books).

- *Finding Hope Again* with Hal Baumchen (Regal Books). Depression and how to overcome it.

- *Released from Bondage* with Judy King and Dr. Fernando Garzon (Thomas Nelson).

- *Freedom in Christ Bible* (Zondervan). A one-year discipleship study with notes in the Bible.

- *Blessed Are the Peacemakers* with Dr. Charles Mylander (Regal Books).

- *A Biblical Guide to Alternative Medicine* with Dr. Michael Jacobson (Regal Books).

- *Setting Your Church Free* with Dr. Charles Mylander (Regal Books).

- *Christ-Centered Therapy* with Dr. Terry and Julie Zuehlke (Zondervan).

The Victory Over the Darkness Series (Regal Books)
- *Overcoming a Negative Self-Image* with Dave Park
- *Overcoming Addictive Behavior* with Mike Quarles
- *Overcoming Doubt*
- *Overcoming Depression*

Youth Books
- *The Bondage Breaker® Youth Edition* with Dave Park (Harvest House)
- *Stomping Out the Darkness* with Dave Park (Regal Books)
- *Stomping Out Fear* with Dave Park and Rich Miller (Harvest House)
- *Stomping Out Depression* with Dave Park (Regal Books)
- *Radical Image** with Dr. Robert Saucy and Dave Park
- *Sold Out for God** with Dr. Robert Saucy and Dave Park
- *Higher Ground** with Dr. Robert Saucy and Dave Park
- *Extreme Faith* with Dave Park (Harvest House)
- *Reality Check* with Rich Miller (Harvest House)
- *Awesome God* with Rich Miller (Harvest House)
- *Real Life** with Dave Park
- *Ultimate Love* with Dave Park (Harvest House)
- *Righteous Pursuit* with Dave Park (Harvest House)
- *Purity Under Pressure* with Dave Park (Harvest House)

*Available directly from Freedom in Christ Ministries only

Contact information for Freedom in Christ Ministries:
9051 Executive Park Drive, Suite 503
Knoxville, TN 37923
Telephone: (865) 342-4000
E-mail: info@ficm.org
Web site: www.ficm.org